Nicho

The Gr

Methuen Drama

Published by Methuen 2006

1 3 5 7 9 10 8 6 4 2

First published in 2006 by
Methuen Publishing Limited
11–12 Buckingham Gate
London SW1E 6LB

Methuen Publishing Limited Reg. No. 3543167

A CIP catalogue record for this book is available from
the British Library

ISBN 0 413 77594 1
978 0 413 77594 8

Typeset by Country Setting, Kingsdown, Kent
Printed and bound in Great Britain by
Bookmarque Ltd, Croydon, Surrey

THE **ABBEY** THEATRE

The Grown-Ups
By Nicholas Kelly

arts
council
ealaíon

The Abbey Theatre gratefully acknowledges the financial support from
the Arts Council/an Chomhairle Ealaíon

The Grown-Ups

By Nicholas Kelly

The Grown-Ups by Nicholas Kelly was first performed at the Peacock Theatre, Dublin on 10 February 2006. Press night was 14 February 2006.

There will be one interval of 15 minutes

Cast (in order of appearance)

Alan	Jonathan Forbes
Nicola	Leigh Arnold
Amy	Fionnuala Murphy
Stephen	Stephen Brennan
Scott	Dan Colley
Director	Gerard Stembridge
Set Designer	Sinead O'Hanlon
Costumes	Suzanne Cave
Sound Designer	Eddie Breslin
Voice Director	Andrea Ainsworth
Company Stage Manager	Stephen Dempsey
Assistant Stage Manager	Elizabeth Gerhardy
Photography	Ros Kavanagh
Graphic Design	Red Dog

Please note that the text of the play which appears in this volume may be changed during the rehearsal process and appear in a slightly altered form in performance.

Biographies

Nicholas Kelly Author

Nicholas's most recent work *The Harmony Suite*, a site-specific documentary play commissioned by Collective Encounters, Liverpool was performed in September 2005. Other stage plays include *A Quiet Life* (commissioned by the Abbey Outreach Department and performed at the Peacock Theatre, 2000), *The Great Jubilee* (Y2K Festival, Fishamble, 2000), *Shapeshifters* (TEAM Theatre Company, 1999), *United Colours of Domino* (Dublin Youth Theatre, 1998) and *The Future is Betamax* (Young Writers' Festival, Royal Court, London, 1996). Radio plays include *The Black Rider* and *Blameless* (RTÉ). He received the P J O'Connor Award for *Blameless* in 1996. Nicholas was Playwright-in-Residence at Project Arts Centre from 2001 to 2003.

Gerard Stembridge Director

Gerard Stembridge directed *Made in China* by Mark O'Rowe and *The Morning after Optimism* by Tom Murphy at the Peacock. He has also directed Shakespeare's *The Comedy of Errors* and his own play, *That Was Then* on the Abbey stage.

Sinead O'Hanlon Set Designer

Sinead studied design in N.C.A.D. and Dun Laoghaire School of Art and Design. After graduating she worked in the Abbey as Design Assistant until 2001. Since then she has worked as a freelance designer for theatre and television. Her previous work includes *Kvetch* (Kilkenny Arts Festival), *The Factory Girls* (Lyric Theatre, Belfast), *Four Stories, Scenes from a Watercooler, Taste* (Gúna Nua), *Candide, The Butterfly Ranch* and *The Yokohama Delegation* (The Performance Corporation), *Dracula* (Samuel Beckett Theatre), *Still* and *Shorts* (Fishamble). Her television work includes *Storylane, The Bandstand, S.M.S.* and *Up for the Match* (RTÉ).

Suzanne Cave Costume Designer

Suzanne graduated in English and Classical Studies from University College Dublin and, after spending several years working in Prague, went on to study Fashion Design at the Grafton Academy, Dublin. Theatre and Opera work includes *One: Healing with Theatre* and *Macbeth-7*, nominated Best Production 2004 Irish Times Theatre Awards (Pan Pan Theatre), *The Four Note Opera* (Opera Theatre Company) and *The Magic Flute* (English Touring Opera). Film and television credits include *Isolation* (Channel

4/Element Films), *Headrush* (Zanzibar Productions), *Conspiracy of Silence* (Littlewing Films, UK), *Love is the Drug* (RTÉ), winner of Best TV Drama at IFTA 2005 and the BAFTA nominated *The Tale of the Rat that Wrote* (Blue Orange Films, UK). Suzanne also works as a stylist for print and TV commercials both in the UK and Ireland. She most recently designed the costumes for *The System* (Project Arts Centre). Suzanne is delighted to be working on her first Abbey/Peacock show.

Kevin McFadden Lighting Designer
Kevin's lighting design credits include *Drama at Inish, What Happened Bridgie Cleary, The Guys* and *A Quiet Life* (Abbey and Peacock Theatres), *Taste, Hamlet* (Gúna Nua), *Romeo and Juliet* (Northside Theatre Company), *Bloody Poetry* (Bank of Ireland Arts Centre) and *Seven Deadly Sins* (Performance Corporation).

Leigh Arnold Nicola
Leigh studied at the American Academy of Dramatic Arts in New York. Her New York theatre credits include *Rose Tobin, The Comedy of Errors, Wrens, Children in Uniform* and *Key Exchange*. She appeared in two series of *The Clinic* in the role of Clodagh Delaney. Leigh is delighted to be making her Irish theatre debut at the Peacock.

Stephen Brennan Stephen
Stephen's most recent appearances at the Abbey Theatre include Tiresias in *The Burial at Thebes*, Noel in *That was Then*, Harry in *The Sanctuary Lamp*, Kearns in *A Life* and Henry in *The Wake*. He spent several years in musicals before joining the Abbey Theatre in 1976, where he played more than sixty leading and supporting roles, including the title role in *Hamlet*. He joined the National Theatre, London in 1983 and apart from Frank'n'Furter in *The Rocky Horror Show* and Petruchio in *The Taming of the Shrew* has worked extensively at the Gate Theatre since 1988. His most recent appearances at the Gate were in *Two Plays After* by Brian Friel, *Old Times* (Pinter Festival) and *A Christmas Carol*. Television includes *Ballykissangel, Father Ted, Bachelors Walk* and *The Big Bow Wow*.

Dan Colley Scott

Dan is currently in his first year at NUI studying Arts. His theatre appearances include *Oliver Twist*, *Waiting for Godot* (US tour, London and Toronto), *As You Like It*, *Cyrano de Bergerac* (Gate Theatre) and *Mutabilitie* (Theatreworks, Samuel Beckett Theatre). His film and television credits include *Foreign Exchange*, *The Big Bow Wow* (RTÉ) *Bloom* and *Reign of Fire*. On radio he played Terry in *All That Fall* (BBC Radio). Dan is delighted to be making his Peacock debut.

Jonathan Forbes Alan

Jonathan's theatre credits include *Romeo and Juliet*, *Hamlet*, *Pontius Pilate*, *King Lear* (RSC), *A View from the Bridge* (Theatr Clwyd) and *A Streetcar Named Desire* (National Theatre, London). Television and film credits include *Hornblower III*, *Conspiracy of Silence*, *The Magnificent Ambersons* and *Mad About Mambo*. Radio includes *Caesar*, *Spring Forward Fall Back*, *Les Miserables*, *Criminal Conversation*, *Get Stuffed*, *Death and the Angel*, *The Day of the Triffids*, *Tasty Morsels* and *Lorenzaccio* (BBC). He received the BBC Carleton Hobbs Award 2001.

Fionnuala Murphy Amy

Fionnuala began acting with Dublin Youth Theatre. Previous productions at the Abbey and Peacock Theatres include *Portia Coughlan*, *Medea*, *Big Maggie*, *The Hunt for Red Willie*, *The Rivals*, *By the Bog of Cats*, *She Stoops to Folly*, *Six Characters in Search of an Author*, *The Only True History of Lizzie Finn*, *The Doctor's Dilemma*, *The Playboy of the Western World*, *The Patriot Game*, *Silverlands*, *The Trojan Women*, *The Broken Jug*, *A Little Like Paradise* and *Playgirl*. Other theatre work includes *The Twelve Pound Look* (Bewleys Café Theatre), *Electra* (b*spoke), *Yerma* (Galloglass), *The Loves of Cass Maguire* (Druid), *The Madame MacAdam Travelling Theatre* (Field Day), *Translations* (Royal Lyceum, Edinburgh), *From Both Hips*, *The Plains of Enna* (Fishamble), *The Government Inspector* (Dubbeljoint), *The Man from Clare*, *The Chastitute* (Gaiety Theatre), *Home*, *Songs of the Reaper* (The Passion Machine) and *Troubled Hearts* (Project Arts Centre). Film and television work includes *The Snapper*, *The Van* and *Agnes Browne*.

THE **ABBEY** THEATRE

Our warmest thanks go to:

Sponsors

Anglo Irish Bank

CityJet

Napa Valley
Vintners

RTÉ

The Irish Times

WRITER-IN-ASSOCIATION
WITH THE ABBEY THEATRE
Conor McPherson

ANGLO
IRISH
BANK

SPONSORED BY
ANGLO IRISH BANK

Benefactors

Allied Irish Bank,
Bankcentre

An Post

Arthur Cox

Bank of Ireland

Behaviour & Attitudes
Marketing Research

Electricity Supply Board

Independent Newspapers
(Ireland) Limited

Irish Life & Permanent Plc

Pfizer International Bank
Europe

SIPTU

Platinum Patrons

Allied Irish Bank,
O'Connell Street

Terry Calvani & Sarah Hill

Lilian & Robert Chambers

Paul and Sheila Grimes

Diageo Ireland

Lorcan Lynch

Mercer Human Resource
Consulting

Andrew & Delyth Parkes

Red Dog

Alan Sheil

Derek Staveley

Adrian Timmons

Total Print & Design

Francis Wintle

Silver Patrons

Joe Byrne

Zita Byrne

Orla Cleary

Maretti D'Arcy

Monica Flood

Paul & Florence Flynn

Francis Keenan

Peter Keenan

Gerard Kelly and Co. Ltd. Builders
Providers

Aisling Kennedy

Matt Knibbs

Paul Leahy

Gary & Bernie Leeson

Mary T. Malone

Padraig Mc Cartan

Mc Cullough Mulvin Architects

Frank & Evelyn Murray

Claire Nolan

Vincent O'Doherty

John P. H. & Rosemary
O' Reilly

Michael Quinn

SIPTU Equity

Michael Slein

Sumitomo Mitsui Finance

Margaret Tallon

Adrian Weller

Members

Ciaran Allen
George Balfe
Kate Bateman
Carmel Clifford &
Francis Barrett
Bobbie Bergin
Philip Bergin
Tony Black
Brendan Bracken
Caroline Brady
Aibhlín Bray
Fiona Breen
Eamon & Deirdre
Brennan
Eilish Brennan
Peig Brightling
Donal Brindley
Francis Britton
Padraig Broe
Joe & Mary Brosnan
Mary Burke
Elizabeth Burke
Kennedy
Rosemary & John Burke
Michael P Butler
Margaret Byrne
Patricia Byrne
Paul Byrne
Margaret Cagney
Imelda Cahill
Hilary Callanan
Ian Campbell
John Campbell
Jennifer Canavan
Eamon & Anne
Cantwell
Georgina Caraher
Maureen Carrigan
Edmund Carton
Mike Casey
Deirdre Cashion
Colin Clarke
Nicola Clarke
Jim & Dympna Clune
Jill Caorke
Anne Cole
Brendan Colgan
Mary - Paula Colgan
Maeve Collins
Paul & Trish Conway
Eileen Connolly
Barry Coonan
Gabriel Conney
Adele Cooper
Tom Corcoran
Sean Copeland
Alan Cox
Catherine Cruise
Leigh Cullen

Gerard Cummiskey
Liz Cunningham
William Cunningham
Maureen Daly
Tom Darragh
Reg Deane
Liam & Antoinette
Deering
Shirley Delahunt
Evin Delaney
Joe Delaney
Patrick Delaney
Anne Desmond
John Devitt
Anne Dolphin
Mrs E. Donaldson
Phelin Donlon
Daibhí Doran
Michael Doran
Rosemaire Dore
Joan Doyle
Eamonn Drea
Anne Duffy
Bernadette Duffy
Orla Duffy
Cora Dunne
Amanda Dunne
Una Dunne
Veronica Edwards
Elizabeth Egan
Anna Envall
Brian Farley
Damien Faron
Pat Farrell
Paul Farrell
Thomas & Linda Farrell
Brian Fenix
Dave Fennell
Tanya Curry &
Ciaran Ferrie
Sean Finlay
Mark Fitzgerald
Mary & Paddy
Fitzgerald
Irene Flynn
James Foley
Andrew Fordham
Charlotte Frorath
Maeve Furlong
Sinead Gallagher
John Gallen
Fiona Galvin
Siobhan Gannon
Finola Geraghty
Sean Geraghty
Simon Geraghty
Penny Gill
Robbie Gilligan
Anne Grace
Jennifer Graniger
Leslie Greer

Roisin Grisfwood
Liam Haines
Grainne Hamilton
Deirdre Hanley
Damien & Marie
Hannan
Gerry Haugh
Don Harris
Bill Harvey
John Hayes
Sandra Heavey
Tom Heneghan
Shay Hennessy
Mary Higgins
Philip Crothers &
Helena Hingston
Annette Holden
Tomás Houlihan
Bernadette Hudson
Adrienne Hughes
Laragh Hughes
Hilary & Suzanne
Humphrys
Monica Hurson Kelly
Roger Hussey
Win Jeffers
Eleanor Jenkins
Mary Jones
Ger Jordan
Ib Jorgensen
Shay Keany
Anne & Tommy Keddy
Jermoe Keliher
Caroline Kelly
Aishling Kennedy
Kieran Kennedy jnr
Marion Kenny
Peter Kerrigan
Brendan & Ger Keogh
Seamus Killeen
Kathleen King
Shona Kinsella
James Lally
Conor Lawlor
Maureen Lehmann
Caroline Lennon
Linda Leonard
Nick Linders
Nuala Long
Keith Lowe
Gabriele Lynch
John Mac Donald
Anthony Mac
Gabhann
Una & Arthur Mac
Manus
Gearoid Mac Unfraidh
Margaret Macken
Eugene Magee
Peter Maher
Ron Maher

Lesley Malone
Julie Manahan
Helen Marks
Frank Marshall
Noel Martyn
John Mc Adam
Michael Mc Cabe
Paul Mc Cabe
Sinead Mc Carthy
Grainne Mc Creevey
Joseph Mc Cullough
Enda Mc Donagh
Ken Mc Donald
Reenagh Mc Donald
Geraldine Mc Donnell
Ian Mc Elligott
John Mc Elligott
Garrett Mc Elroy
Lauren Mc Garry
Anna Mc Gillicuddy
John Mc Glade
Bernie Mc Grath
Moira Mc Hugh
Brian Mc Kiernan
Clare Mc Mahon
Ross Mc Parland
Berna Mc Menamin
Emer Mc Sweeney
Rita Mc Sweeney
Patrick Merrigan
Patricia Miller
Brid Milton
Paul Mitchell
Patrick Molloy
Eve Molony
Donie Mooney
Frank Mooney
John Paul Mooney
Tom Mooney
Jenny Moran
Paul Moran
Anne Morris
Liam Mulaney
Jane Mulcahy
Monica Mulholland
Claire Murphy
Elaine Murphy
John Murphy
John Murphy
Marian Murphy
Michelle Murphy
Patrick F Murphy
Frances & William
Murray
Maureen Murray
Noeleen Murray
Margaret Myron
Jedel Naidoo
Carmel Naughton
Geraldine Naughton
Kevin Nealon

Marie Ni
Mhaoilmhichil
Úna Ní Shúilleabháin
Giuliano Nistri
Tony Neville
Kathleen Nolan
Emma Jane Nulty
Aishling O'Beirne
Siobhan O'Beirne
Olivia O'Boyle
Geraldine O'Brien
Eibhlín & Séan O'Broin
Séamus O'Cinnéide
Catherine O'Connor
Mary O'Connor
PJ & Helen O'Connor
Tom O'Connor
Ethel O'Dea
Pauric O'Doherty
Padriag O'Domhaill
Frances O'Donnell
James O'Donnell
Mary O'Donnell
Philomena O'Dowd
Mary O'Driscoll
Ronan O'Driscoll
Marc O'Dwyer
Ciara O' Farrell
Colette O'Farrell
Diarmuid O'Fatharta
Pol O Gallichcoir
Micheál & Máire
O'Gruagáin
Mrs. Billy O'Hara
Lilian O'Kane
Brenda & Peter O'Leary
Edel O'Leary
Michael V O'Mahony
Fionan
O'Muircheartaigh
Donnacadh O'Neill
Susan O'Neill
Fiona O'Regan
Helen O'Rourke
Mary O'Rourke
Roger O'Shea
Anne & Eileen
O'Sullivan
Ian O'Sullivan
Tara O'Sullivan
Valerie O'Toole
Ruth Payne
Brother James Pidgeon
Pauline Power
Sharon Power
Ian Price
Antoinette Quinn
Heather Quinn
Michele Quinn
Chris Rayner
Denis Reen

Mr & Mrs A Reid
Yvonne Reilly
Eadaoin Rennick
Mary Reynolds
Charles Richards
Laurence Roe
Eamon & Maura Rohan
Margaret Rooney
Patrick D Rowan
Nike Ruf
Beatrice Ryan
Sinead Ryan
Gillian Saunders
Oliver Schubert
Emir Shanahan
Maura Sheehy
Nicola Sherry
Ann Simmons
Margaret Skeffington
Graham Smith
Brian & Lyndall Smyth
Nell Snow
Ann & Christy Stenson
Martina Stenson
Orla Sutton
Rita Sweeney
Gerard Thunder
Greg Tierney
Simon Tierney
Deidre Tobin
Lisa Toner
Anne-Marie Trenaman
Adrian Tucker
Yvonne Tuohy
Bronagh Twomey
Violet Ui Dulaing
Priti Jane Varma
Michael Wall
Lesley Wallace
Pauline Walley SC
Noreen Walls
James Walsh
John Walsh
Sarah Walsh
Tony Wann
Fiona Whelan
Lorraine Whelan
Noreen Whelan
Catherine Williams
Brendan Williams
John & Siobhan
Woodhouse
Conor Wynne
Wade Wyse
Corrie Zemann-Dolan

Abbey Staff

BOARD

Eithne Healy - Chairman
Loretta Brennan Glucksman
Siobhán Bourke
Eugene Downes
Paul Mercier
Niall O'Brien
John O'Mahony
Michael J. Somers
John Stapleton

Director
Fiach Mac Conghail

Director of Finance and Administration
Declan Cantwell

Literary Director
Aideen Howard

Director of Public Affairs
Janice McAdam (Acting)

Director of Technical Services and Operations
Tony Wakefield

ARTISTIC

Abbey Players
Des Cave

Anglo Irish Bank Writer-in-Association
Conor McPherson

Associate Artists
David Gothard
Paul Keogan
Conall Morrison
Bairbre Ní Chaoimh

Honorary Associate Directors
Vincent Dowling
Tomás MacAnna

Casting
Marie Kelly

Executive Office
Orla Mulligan

Voice Director
Andrea Ainsworth

FINANCE AND ADMINISTRATION

Accounts
Robert Hogan
Suzanne Lowe
Pat O'Connell

Human Resources
Keira Matthews

Information Technology
Ivan Kavanagh
Dave O'Brien

LITERARY

Archive
Mairéad Delaney

Literary
Aoife Habenicht

PUBLIC AFFAIRS

Box Office
Des Byrne
Catherine Casey
Clare Downey
Anne Marie Doyle
Sonia Gamble
Lorraine Hanna
Marie Claire Hoysted
Iain Mullins
Maureen Robertson

Development
Áine Kiernan

Front of House
John Baynes
Stephen Brennan
David Clarke
Roisin Coyle
Stephen Coyne
Con Doyle
Adam Doyle
Sinead Flynn
Neil Gallagher
Joanna Kaczor
Conor Matthews
Dominik Neinart

Characters

Alan Simms
Nicola Klyne
Amy Simms
Stephen
Scott

Setting

An apartment in a city. Later, a back room in a bar.

Time

Summer, the present.

Act One

Darkness. A gentle breeze, birdsong.

Lights up first on a very specific part of the stage: a balcony area which is created by four faux-Doric columns. Lush golden light (a sundown, presumably) bathes the floor. A plant pot sits luxuriously on a low, white plinth. Beside the plant there's a packet of cigarettes and a lighter. Where are we? Who knows?

*Standing between the columns is a young man of thirty called **Alan Simms**. He is staring at something in his hand with an oddly detached, faintly bemused expression. What's in his hand? It is a set of keys, attached to a large – and rather unusual – key chain. Perhaps it is a heavy blue globe or an oversized, swirling marble. Whatever it is, it should be highly distinctive – and shiny.*

Lights up to full revealing the rest of the stage – we're actually in a spacious one-bedroom apartment. The balcony seems to fit with the overall 'design': bare white walls, cracking in places, earthy wooden floorboards. The sparse but well chosen furniture is similarly restrained. A dining table, set for two. On the dining table is a candelabra, lying on its side.

Oddly, however, tendrils of lush, green ivy have begun to grow down from the 'ceiling', clinging perhaps to a partially built wall, which could suggest the perimeter of the building. There's something odd about this – is it a design feature or nature invading?

***Nicola Klyne** comes on, in some kind of business suit. She cuts quite a dash: dynamic, slim, sexy – the confident, professional woman. She's about twenty-five. She watches **Alan** a moment: he has his back turned to her.*

Nicola   The coffee stains on my teeth. You think I should get them bleached?

***Alan** pockets the keys, unseen. He turns to **Nicola**. She shrugs, a little embarrassed.*

Alan *(appearing casual)*   The coffee stains on your *teeth?* What coffee stains?

Nicola (*amused*)   He says there's no coffee stains. Of course, you'd pretend not to notice. (*Beat.*) I see the table is set. How are you – psyched?

Alan (*laughs*)   Well, I'm psyched as I can be. Run along, run along.

Nicola (*amused*)   'Run along'?

Alan   It's an expression!

Nicola   Oh, now. I don't know. Since you've said 'run along', I am sorely tempted to stay. What's the deal here? You going to light a few candles?

Alan (*shrugs*)   I thought about it.

Nicola (*amused*)   You wanna try make the place all . . . atmospheric, is that your game, buster? It's your sister, you know. And also, given the context . . .

Alan   Fair point.

He goes over and picks up the candelabra. He brings it to a cabinet.

Nicola (*laughs, a little troubled*)   Candles, I swear. I mean, what are you like?

Alan *puts the candelabra in the cabinet. He has a thought. Unseen by* **Nicola***, he takes the keys from his jacket pocket. He considers throwing them into the cabinet. He changes his mind and re-pockets them. He turns to her.*

Alan   Scoot! I'll survive here.

Nicola   Now, there's no need to fret. We still have plenty of time. (*Shrugs.*) And, well, I dunno, I wouldn't mind a quick look at her.

Alan (*grimly*)   There'll be time for that. You can come see her in *court*. You can see her face, Nicola, when it's splashed over the papers . . . mine, too, most likely, unless I'm careful. (*Sighs.*) Richard's already told me he finds this 'distasteful'. The fact that I work there and Amy, she . . . (*Sighs, beat.*) Did I tell you that, did I? That he used that precise word?

Nicola (*sighs*) Only about two thousand times.

Alan Well, what *I'd like to know* is what's so distasteful about it? (*Shrugs*.) Amy, now, granted – should the story be true. But what does the man think? I'm gonna freak out as well?

Nicola (*looks at him a moment, quietly*) Alan.

Alan Hmm?

Nicola Just what did you mean back there? In the bathroom, I mean. What did you mean to infer when you so casually asked . . . ? (*Sighs*.) When you asked me if Richard would take me for a spin?

Alan Nothing!

Nicola Nothing.

Alan Not at all! That was just . . . off the cuff; it was . . . conversation. (*Laughs*.) You're meeting Richard tonight, yes? You're meeting Richard, his friend; this business acquaintance. (*Shrugs*.) Well, I thought maybe *Richard*, since he's got these new wheels, well, I thought that he might . . . (*Beat, laughs*.) You know Richard, love: the guy's a complete show-off.

Nicola (*doubtful*) Right.

Alan What we're talking about here is the word 'distasteful'. *That's* what has me concerned. (*Shrugs*.) Naturally, of course, I'm worried about Amy.

Nicola How's my hair?

Alan (*trying to be casual*) Richard, of course . . . well, we're all friends here, right?

Nicola *scowls. She closes her eyes. She turns away.*

Alan (*feigning innocence*) What?

Nicola You know what.

Alan *What?*

Nicola You know what. (*Frustrated*.) You cannot possibly tell me that this doesn't irk you. You cannot possibly suggest . . .

(*Beat.*) Okay, then, buster, you want to play it that way. This is probably not the right time for this discussion, I know that, but I'm terribly sorry, it's been bugging me all evening. Now, I *fully support* your plan of action. I am fully behind you. Because, of course, it's only natural that you would be concerned about your sister in all this . . . but as regards *Richard*, that's a different story, now, isn't it? I think we both know that you two have your differences. And I think that it's plain – no matter how much you protest – what the real reason is why you and he have never really seemed to get on. (*Sighs.*) So, this kid – you said 'Scott' – he's landed Amy right in it. So, Richard, it appears, is standing by him . . .

Alan   We get on great. It was just that comment . . .

Nicola   Oh, don't be such a child, Alan, it's written all over your face. You're just itching for the chance to have a row with him, aren't you? You're dying for it – I mean, we both know why – and, well, the truth, since you must know, the truth is: *enough*. I don't want to come back tonight and have you quizzing me. I'm tired of this saga about Richard Carlisle; how he looked at you cross-eyed, or those kids in the bar, see? Because I think we both know that your problem's with *me*.

They look at one another. This strikes a chord. **Alan** *turns away.*

Nicola   I know that you've said that your sister has problems. I know you must feel obliged to leap into the fray . . . but please don't use it as a weapon to try and hit back at me. (*Scowls.*) Richard and I: that's ancient history. And so what's the big swing if I fell from grace once, huh? We were broken up, weren't we? It was only that one time. It was only that one time and you said you were fine with it; what do you want me to do, never see him again? He puts work my way, doesn't he? I have a life; I have . . . debts . . .

She sighs. She's said enough. She's embarrassed now.

Look, I've changed my mind on these shoes. Just give me a second, will you?

Alan (*approaching her*)   Nicola, I . . .

Nicola   You need to quit this, all right? You need to get a grip, and if you can't, well, we're . . . (*Beat, sighs.*) Now that your sister's involved, I can see it all getting nasty.

She looks at him a moment. She goes off.

Alan (*calling after her, defensively*)   When I mentioned his car . . . that was just conversation!

He scowls. He takes out the keys. He looks for somewhere to hide them.

Nicola *comes back on, carrying a pair of shoes.*

Alan   So. We're done fighting?

Nicola (*putting her shoes on*)   It's adolescent behaviour. And you never mentioned my hair.

Alan   It's lovely. It's . . . chic.

Nicola *looks at him a moment. She seems satisfied. But something is still troubling him.*

Alan   My *professional* problem is with those kids in the bar.

Nicola (*shrugs*)   So, be assertive.

Alan   I discussed the matter with him. And Richard, he seems . . . well, he's just so . . . blasé.

Nicola (*rising*)   Look, I better make tracks. We can talk when I get home, yeah?

Alan   Those kids who come down, they can't be more than sixteen, can they? They're completely conceited. They think the world's there to please them. Now, all of this has kicked off since Jonathan went to Karlovy Vari. It's the fact that he – Richard – well, he serves those kids, doesn't he? Now, sure, that's okay: we all turn a blind eye sometimes. But now I hear that my sister, she's been accused of . . .

Nicola   Talk to her.

Alan   I will. I intend to. Nicola, I . . . before you go. (*Beat.*) Just tell me, okay, what you make of this, right? Be honest with me, there's no double-meanings. This customer comes in. Our first since the flood. Now, Richard didn't twig – he's never met my sister – but I recognised the guy, it was Amy's *boyfriend*, okay? Stephen's his name, she introduced me to him yesterday. Now, Stephen and Amy, they've only been together a few months, but if you ask me, he's . . . (*Awkwardly, laughs.*) Well, if Stephen's banging my *sister*, the guy must have a screw loose. Anyway, it was just before lunchtime and Stephen saunters in, he's already jarred. I ducked out of sight, I mean, I thought it best. Now, I don't really know what he was doing in the place, maybe he was looking for me, but Richard, of course, he shows Stephen the door, he tells him he's well on. (*Irritated.*) After he's gone, Richard comes up to me. He's completely polite, love. This is what he says. 'Alan, I've a hunch that that one might be trouble. Don't let him in if he comes back here, okay?'

Nicola (*lost*)   So?

Alan   Well, don't you think that perhaps there's something weird about that?

Nicola *shrugs. She turns to go.*

Alan (*a little frantic*)   Look, sweetheart, I swear: I'm not trying to punish you. I'm not angry with you, or with Richard or anyone. I just want to know what Amy's messed up in. These kids keep coming and going. Now, Stephen's on the scene. (*Beat.*) I feel like I'm out of the loop here. Can't you cut me some slack?

Nicola *sighs. She turns back to him.*

Nicola (*a little sadly*)   You really think that she did it?

Alan (*without looking at her*)   I think it's certainly possible. Amy, she . . . (*Beat.*) The woman can be irrational. (*Laughs.*) When she was sixteen, seventeen, no one could say 'boo' to her. There was a problem at home, she'd go missing for days. (*Laughs.*) As regards this fiasco with her teaching those people, I . . . (*Shrugs.*) Well, I could certainly see her losing her cool, yes.

Nicola   I'm sorry if it seemed like I went over the top back there.

Alan   I mean, I tried to broach it at the coffee place yesterday. I know she hangs out there; she spends her life in that place.

I'd barely got down to the 'How are you, Amy?' and 'Crazy weather we're having', before that boyfriend of hers – Stephen's on the case. He slips in beside us, he has this look in his eyes. What could I do? I couldn't discuss it then. (*A little overwhelmed.*) So, I said come for dinner, I had to do something . . . (*Beat.*) Richard has seen that kid's bruises. (*Laughs.*) She doesn't know that I know. I mean, Amy's no clue that we're even acquainted.

Amy *comes on. She's about thirty-five. She is not the fearsome presence we may have imagined. She is wearing a rather uninspiring ensemble: a drab pair of trousers, an eccentric thrift-store top. A shoulder-bag. She sees* **Nicola** *first, and almost collides with her.*

Amy   Oh!

Nicola   Hey!

Amy   You – ?

Nicola   And you must be Amy. Nicola, hi. Oh, don't worry, don't worry, I was on my way out. I wouldn't want for a second to get in the way here!

Amy (to **Alan**)   Your buzzer's broken, it seems. Didn't you hear me knocking? Be bold, I thought, swan right on through.

Alan   Hello, Amy.

Amy   I'm his big sister.

Nicola   So we all gathered. (*Laughs nervously.*) Well, I would *definitely* say that there's some resemblance! (*Unsure, to* **Alan**.) Okay, then, cool. Shall I leave you pair to it?

Amy (*looking about*)   Now, that's the exact thing I was thinking earlier today. Isn't that just bizarre? Of course, I was going to ring and *confirm* the arrangement, but then I thought you'd conclude that I was somehow insane. (*Laughs.*) I couldn't quite fathom if the invitation . . . I wasn't sure if the *four*, I mean, you two, and Stephen . . . (*Sighs.*) Anyway, the point is moot, Stephen's indisposed. The man is unwell, Alan. Just a twenty-four-hour thing. But that was insane of me, wasn't it, because the table's only set for *two*.

Alan *and* **Nicola** *look at one another. Both seem a little shell-shocked.*

A phone rings.

Nicola (*brightly*)   I've a head like a sieve: I forgot my phone.

Alan *finds* **Nicola**'s *mobile phone.*

Nicola   Anyhow, Amy, I hate to run out like this. We'll meet again, surely. (*Approaching* **Alan**, *awkwardly.*) He's been cooking for you, Amy; the boy's been slaving all evening . . .

Alan *offers* **Nicola** *the phone.*

Alan   Nicola.

Nicola   Cheers.

Alan   It's Richard.

Nicola (*to* **Amy**)   These high-fliers, you know, they can't amuse themselves for ten seconds. Well, I'll see you guys later. Enjoy!

She takes the phone. She goes off.

Amy   So, what's got her spooked?

Alan   Spooked? She's not spooked. She has a work gig, that's all. I thought that the two of us . . .

Amy   She seems nice. A bit thin.

Alan   Wine?

Amy   I apologise, of course, if I'm a little bit late here. I didn't dress up, see? I wasn't sure if I should. (*Laughs.*) I'm a bit spooked here myself.

Alan   Why are you spooked, Amy?

Amy   Out of the blue, you turn up at the coffee place? Now, that in itself was *a bombshell*. You wouldn't believe what was whirling around in here. My first thought, of course, was that something had happened to Mammy. And now tonight I'm *in situ* . . . your lovely lady . . . the crib . . . (*Grandly.*) This is setting a precedent. It is strange. And auspicious.

Alan   You're looking . . . well.

Amy (*amused*) 'Well'? Do you think? (*Beat.*) Coming up in the world, then. That much is plain. Mammy told me, of course, you'd been lucky in love. (*Looking about the apartment.*) You know, I have to be honest: I'm pleasantly surprised here. What was I expecting? I don't know what I was expecting. A TV, perhaps, the size of a billboard. A Salvador Dali print on the wall. Or a Gustav Klimt. Not, to suggest, of course, that I'd question your taste . . .

Alan Why don't you sit down, Amy? Let me get you a drink.

Amy (*a little more relaxed*) Stephen's chuffed, by the way.

Alan Chuffed?

Amy To the gills. Positively radiant, despite being ill. He thinks it's unnatural when families are estranged. (*Laughs.*) Naturally I explained, we're an unnatural family . . . but he seems to have faith in you. (*Laughs.*) Faith in the man and he's only known him ten minutes! (*Looking at* **Alan** *more closely.*) Stephen thinks you might be having a quarter-life crisis. He thinks that explains this . . . reaching out . . . (*Laughs.*) Well, I said to Stephen, 'Quarter-life crisis? The man must be thirty.' (*Shrugs.*) But each to their own: we all grow at a pace . . .

Alan (*looks at her a moment, overwhelmed*) Amy?

Amy Huh?

Alan If there's something you . . . I mean, are you sure you're all right?

Amy (*laughs nervously*) Well, who's the one having the quarter-life crisis here, pal? (*Beat.*) I'm fair to middling as ever. But you think I'm barking mad, don't you?

Alan *looks at her. He can't win. He gives her wine. They look at one another.*

Amy What? (*Alarmed.*) Is there something . . . ?

Nicola *comes on, with the phone.*

Nicola Okay, now, folks, bit of a disaster. Richard, he . . . (*Cautiously.*) A colleague of mine . . . he's left me high and dry, see? Now, he wouldn't say why, and, folks, it's a bit rich . . . (*She puts her phone down.*) Embarrassing, isn't it? I'll try not to intrude.

She goes off.

Alan (*grimly, to self*)   Can't even call for a cab, then?

Amy   She's just going to lurk back there, is she? While we tuck into dinner? (*Laughs.*) I don't mean to be rude here, but if there's some kind of agenda, I'd like to be kept in the loop. (*Beat.*) I thought that you said you wanted me to meet her. I thought *that* was the purpose . . . I should have rung and confirmed.

Alan   Excuse me a second. I need to check the food.

Amy   No problem.

Alan *looks at her a moment. He goes off.*

Amy   My God. It's a nightmare.

She sighs heavily. She grips her glass of wine. She knocks it back in one go. She takes a deep breath.

Okay. Okay. (*Steeling herself.*) Okay, no problem. (*Laughs, breezy.*) An automatic response, that's all it is. *Automatically*, I . . . (*Laughs.*) You see, my glass is half-empty!

But she hasn't convinced herself. She picks up her empty wine glass and goes in search of the bottle.

Damn it to hell. (*Beat.*) I could do a runner.

Alan (*off*)   Won't be a second now, Amy.

Amy (*breezy again*)   Oh, there's no rush, my man. I've found the bottle now anyway. (*Approaching an exit, regarding the ivy.*) So, is this is the latest fad? (*Drinking the wine.*) I think I sort of like it. (*Shrugs.*) It's decadent, of course. But then, everything is these days. Did you get like a – what? – a landscape architect or somebody? (*Approaching the exit.*) I said, did one of those, Alan, those green-fingered people – ?

Nicola *comes on.*

Amy (*in fright*)   Oh!

Nicola   Did I startle you? Oops. The kitchen's over there.

Amy *turns in confusion. She looks about the room.* **Nicola** *considers going off again. But she sighs and turns back – it would be rude for her to go.*

Nicola   I mean, I know what you're thinking: it's a bit rough and ready, right? We wanted the space, though. Plus, I'm freelancing mostly, so we couldn't really afford anything too extravagant. (*Laughs.*) We shall freeze come the winter. But the rent's not too bad. (*Beat.*) Renting? You're renting?

Amy   Oh, I'm renting.

Nicola (*laughs nervously*)   You're renting these days, people think there's something wrong with you.

They look at one another. Both smile nervously.

Alan *comes on, with condiments. He is surprised to see* **Nicola**. *He goes straight to her.*

A shadow flits across the balcony – a bird perhaps?

Nicola (*sotto voce, to* **Alan**)   You want my opinion, you shouldn't pussyfoot around here. The poor woman's in tatters: she almost leapt out of her skin.

Alan *and* **Nicola** *turn to look at* **Amy**.

Nicola (*brightly, to* **Amy**)   Bye now!

She goes off.

Silence.

Alan   So?

Amy   Yes?

Alan   How's the . . . teaching?

Stephen *stumbles on, breathless. He's about fifty. He is rather dishevelled.* **Amy** *and* **Alan** *look at him a moment.*

Amy   Stephen.

Alan   Stephen!

Amy   Well, there we are: it's my bedraggled knight.

Alan (*completely thrown*)   Uh, Nicola, come out. Stephen is here.

Stephen (*finally catching his breath*)   The story's long-winded. I hope I'm not interrupting.

Amy looks at Stephen a moment. She shakes her head, exasperated.

Amy (*to Alan*)   Bathroom?

Alan *points her to it.* **Amy** *goes off.*

Alan   Anyhow, Stephen, great to see you again. (*Awkwardly.*) You found the place, did you? She gave you the address? (*At a loss.*) Amy tells me you're chuffed that I . . . (*Awkwardly.*) Well, she said you were ill, Stephen, you've kind of thrown me for six here . . .

Smoke begins to waft gently on to the stage.

(*Laughs, removing his jacket.*) Look, unfortunately, Stephen, I wasn't really expecting you. There's not exactly much food, see, although I suppose we could manage. (*Beat.*) Smoke? You smell smoke?

Nicola *comes on. She has changed her clothes into something more casual.*

Nicola   I think I smell smoke here.

Alan   Smoke! (*To* **Nicola**.) Some assistance!

He throws his jacket to the floor. **Alan** *and* **Nicola** *go off.*

Stephen (*amused*)   Tremendous.

He looks about. He sees the ivy. He looks up at it. He's amused.

(*Cheerfully.*) Seems I've arrived in the thick of it.

He goes to the table. He picks up the bottle of wine, inspects the label, and pours himself a glass.

Amy *comes on. She seems different . . . she's been smoking pot, actually.*

Stephen *looks at her, smiles.*

Stephen   Well, I think we can safely say that that – (*He indicates the ivy.*) – is unusual. (*He takes a drink. Regarding the ivy.*) It's a mutation, if you ask me. It worms its way from the outside, burrows in through the cracks; and, thus, then, you see, with the right conditions . . .

Amy   Oh, Lord, he must know. What are you doing here, anyway?

Stephen (*laughs*)   What am I doing here? Why should I know what I'm doing here? You did invite me, my love.

Amy   Then where were you at seven thirty? By the clock?

Stephen (*shrugs*)   I was detained. You might have lingered.

Amy (*laughs*)   Linger? Out there? I'm not going to linger. (*Laughs.*) So now, I *have* to linger for the malingerer here. (*Sighs.*) Regardless, it's moot because it turns out I was wrong. If you *had* been invited, you'd have gone AWOL. (*Laughs, in wonder.*) Let's hear the excuse, then. Run into a buddy? Thought you'd repair for a swift one?

Stephen (*affectionately*)   You're stoned.

Amy   Well, of course I'm stoned now, pal! Of course I'm stoned now. Just how am I supposed to maintain a degree of semblance . . . ? Oh, he knows, oh he knows! (*Sighs.*) I sparked up in the bathroom. (*A sudden thought, alarmed.*) You mean, Lord, is it obvious?

Stephen   How do you know that he knows?

Amy   Because he knows, oh, he must. There was a look on his face; he even asked me about teaching. Why would he ask me? Didn't I tell him at coffee that I finished up last week?

Stephen   Maybe it slipped his mind.

Amy (*scowls*)   I told him you were ill, you know. The next minute, you're . . . manifest. (*Frustrated, looking through her bag.*) Oh, sometimes I think every one of my problems . . . !

She finds a hairbrush. She begins to brush her hair, while pacing the room.

Stephen (*casually*)   May I explain why I was late now?

Amy   He knows! (*Doubtful.*) He believes it? (*Laughs.*) That would be typical of him, wouldn't it? Oh, that's par for the course, jumping straight to conclusions . . .

Stephen   If you'll indulge me, my sweet. I bring new developments.

Amy   You do?

Stephen   I would think so.

Amy   Well, go on.

Stephen *just smiles at her.* **Amy** *becomes impatient. She puts her hairbrush away. She folds her arms.*

Stephen   Now, do I have your attention? Splendid. (*He looks off, approaches her.*) Well, as I told you this morning, I said I'd delve a bit, didn't I? (**Amy** *sighs.*) Hold on, hold on. Until you hear my petition. (*Beat.*) I took out the map, love. Taking that school as the centre, I drew a quadrangle, a square mile, here or there; bounded to the north by the river, to the south by the overpass. I explored the territory. On foot, but of course there'd been the flood, as you know, and folk were still mopping up. I took it upon myself, from early morning till eve, to make sure I'd frequented every pub, every alehouse . . .

Amy *scowls.*

Stephen   Will you please just indulge me, will you please, will you please? (*Beat.*) Now, I didn't stop for a drink in every single establishment. (*Laughs.*) I mean, if that were the case I'd have had about forty-five pints! (*Sadly.*) By mid-afternoon, I was feeling very dispirited. And none the wiser, it seemed – I mean, I didn't even know what I was looking for. I'd seen much sadness those hours. Jaded team-leaders getting frisky on cocktails. Pale, busty, blondes, looking winsome, forlorn. (*Laughs.*) Oh, come another five years, they'll regret those tattoos, huh? (*Sighs.*) Anyhow, love, I had all but decided to chuck in the wet towel and make my way up to meet you, when I passed by The Wren and I thought I'd give it the once-over. You know

The Wren, don't you? I know the head barman, he's a buddy of mine. (*Beat.*) And lo and behold, as if the gods were at last smiling, standing there at the counter, tapping his foot . . . (*Beat.*) A certain calibre of . . . youth.

Amy (*horrified*)   It was . . . Scott?

Stephen   He didn't fit the description of your nemesis, no.

Amy's *relieved.*

Stephen   However, however. There were certain, irrefutable . . . similarities. He was conceited, of course. But he also held himself rather stiffly. One hand in the sports jacket, a big bag on the bar-top. He's drinking, I think, it looked like fortified wine. His hair is immaculate: black, goes straight up. (*Laughs.*) And eighteen, my eye, Amy.

Amy (*looking off*)   Looks like it's code-red in there. He'll need to change tactics now.

Stephen   I make my approach, doing my best to seem casual. I take a stool by the boy. Oh, The Wren never changes. Now, the first thing I notice is the book, you see, dear. In his bag, on the bar-top, shoved into the back flap . . . well, it was a journal, a handbook . . .

Amy   From the school?

Stephen (*grimly*)   The Advanced Institution for Educational Enrichment. (*Beat.*) Now, I know what you're thinking. There are surely *some* nice boys and girls that have enrolled in that school, yes? True. Very true. His sense of . . . style struck a chord, though. And that obnoxious air of self . . . satisfaction that seemed to ring through every nuance, every gesture. I order a stout. The kid's mobile phone rings. He pulls out the handset, he puts the wine down. Gives me the once-over and starts yammering, doesn't he? Well, at this point, my love, I should have been bursting my tits. I should have been on my way, also . . . but bear with me, bear with me. Underneath this façade . . . was a quality to him, a kind of savage . . . desperation. I know what it is with desperation these days. I can just smell it . . . and this boy, he . . . (*Beat.*) Well, he's

yammering on about the 21st of June. The 21st is approaching,
the fact seems to fill him with dread. As if life, as we know it,
was going to end at midsummer. I can't quite make it all out,
and the child has noticed me watching now, but the *venom*, my
love, well, frankly, I . . . (*He is overwhelmed.*) The kid snaps shut
the handset. I see the whites of his eyes. Now all the while I'm
trying to keep cool here. He swears. He seems to . . . shudder.
So, I give him the *spiel* – 'Looks like you've had a hard day
there.' I mean, as we all know, I have a way with these people.
'That weather,' says I. He refuses to play. Well, it seemed to
me, I was going nowhere fast, so what the devil, I thought,
I shall just have it out. I put my hand on his arm. I feel him
stiffen. I say to the lad, 'June 21st, eh?'

Amy   And?

Stephen   Well, the little skite whirls around and tries to
punch me in the face!

Nicola *comes on with another bottle of wine.*

Nicola (*brightly*)   Everybody sorted for wine, then? It's a nice
Chardonnay.

Amy (*a little thrown, to* **Nicola**)   Oh. Thanks a million. (*Sotto
voce.*) He did what? He hit you?

Nicola   Anyhow, folks, there's been a bit of a rethink. Alan's
decided . . . well, I'm up-for-people, and now Stephen's here . . .
(*Laughs, feigning conviviality.*) I made it explicit, I have eaten
already . . . (*Beat.*) A pleasure to meet you. Nicola Klyne.

She shakes **Stephen***'s hand. She turns away. She notices* **Alan***'s jacket
on the floor. She reaches for it.*

Nicola   He just flings his gear anywhere!

She picks up **Alan***'s jacket. The keys fall out of the pocket. She bends
down. She picks them up. She looks at them strangely a moment. She
hangs* **Alan***'s jacket up somewhere. She goes off, with the keys.*

Amy   This is actually *happening*. We're going to have to sit
through his cooking now. (*Beat.*) So, what . . . ? So, what
happened?

Stephen   I'm knocked to the ground, darling. The barman speeds around. Now, thankfully, the kid only caught me with a glancing blow, but the boy's looming over, it looks like he'll lay into me. The barman pulls him back. The boy shoves the barman. (*Heavily.*) And, well . . . with an emphatic usage of that old favourite, the F-word, the boy grabs his bag, and he high-tails it out of there. Out on to the streets, to wreak havoc, I figure . . .

Amy (*looks at* **Stephen** *in despair*)   I mean, why can't I get through the day without something awful happening? Why can't I get through the day, just the once . . . just the once . . . What is with *wrong* with these people? What is wrong, is it the drink . . . ? (*Scowls.*) Alan asked me again, how teaching was going, even though I clearly stated I had finished up last week. That must mean, he . . . (*Sighs.*) Oh, then, it'll get back to Mammy, and there's no chance she'll believe me . . .

Stephen   This June 21st thing mean anything to you, then?

Amy   No. No, it doesn't. (*Lost.*) You think my kid and your kid, you think there's some connection?

Stephen   Well, they both go to that school, don't they? I would think, at the very least, it's worth pursuing further.

Amy   Yes. You could be right. But that hardly explains why Scott, he . . .

She sighs. She looks off.

Stephen   Look, if you want my opinion: you should just tell Alan what happened.

Amy (*exasperated*)   And what would be the point in that, Stephen? He's hardly going to believe me. And, then, you know . . . the whole story will come out, and either way, I'm in disgrace again, aren't I? I end up just looking like an incompetent . . . misfit, and there's no way on this earth I'll give him that satisfaction. (*Beat.*) He can't know. He can't. There's been nothing in the papers yet, and sooner or later this will just all go away. (*Laughs.*) It's a . . . teacup, now, isn't it? I've blown it all out of proportion . . .

Stephen *takes her in his arms. She sighs deeply, but welcomes the embrace.*

Amy (*breaks away, can't take any more*)   Let's do a runner!

Nicola and **Alan** *come on: they are carrying an assortment of dishes: pasta, a salad bowl, a basket of bread, etc.* **Nicola** *is in a foul mood. She is carrying a glass of wine and is already quite tipsy.*

Stephen (*as if in mid-stream*)   Or a little bird, even. A tiny little bird – say a thrush, for example – sails in through the window, a seed in its mouth. Deposits the said seed and, as the kids say, 'result' –

Alan   What's that, Stephen?

Stephen *points to the ivy.*

Alan   Oh, yeah, the big mystery. We really need to attend to that. (*Claps his hands.*) Anyway, look, apologies all round for the pretty late start here. (*Feigning a joke.*) So, that's two late arrivals we've had this evening. Nice to see you again, Stephen, you're very welcome. Let's sit down, sit down.

They gather at the table.

(*Noticing* **Amy**'s *distress.*) You okay?

Amy   I'm ecstatic.

Nicola   Now, I'll just sit down and join you for ten minutes or so, yeah? Let you all carry on with it. (*Sitting down, to* **Stephen**.) I suppose that I owe you an explanation. I had a prior engagement, you see. It was quite important, to be honest . . . a colleague, you see, a very good friend of our good friend, Richard . . . (*Scowls.*) Well, I was hoping that the colleague – he's a management consultant, and I was hoping that maybe he would put some work my way, okay? (*Laughs.*) I got my hair done and all – this is more than you need here.

Alan   We have chick peas. Tuna. Chives. They are *pfifferlinge* mushrooms, a little . . . *chargrilled*, I'm afraid. A warm walnut bread. A herb salad . . .

Stephen (*reaching for food*)   Mind if I . . . ?

All sit. Dishes are exchanged.

Nicola   Anyhow, Stephen, I don't mean to harp on here . . . (*With a look to* **Alan**.) I don't mean to harp, but I'm going to harp anyway. It's only been the past month that my career's started to kick off. I had a false start, you see. I mean, since we're on the subject, I might as well tell you that, too. (*Laughs.*) You are looking at it, folks: an ex-flight attendant. An air hostess, me, would you ever believe it? Anyhow, unsurprisingly enough, I got tired of being treated like some kind of . . . invertebrate, so I went and I got myself the diploma in marketing. (*Glaring at* **Alan**.) I mostly freelance right now. It's my bread and butter.

Alan (*nervous laughter*)   Okay, calm down, there's been a misunderstanding.

Nicola   Misunderstanding?

Alan   Aren't you going to eat?

Nicola   *Misunderstanding?* You swore you weren't trying to punish me!

Alan (*trying for a joke, to the others*)   It's a misunderstanding, that's all. My boss down the bar, Richard . . . well, he's kind of her boss, too, see? Would-be-boss, anyway – he puts some stuff her way. Now I found his car keys, I forgot to mention it, that's all. Nicola's . . . rattled, because she thinks I . . . (*Laughs, to* **Nicola**.) I mean, seriously, love, it's not like I did it to spite him.

Nicola (*laughs*)   Oh, that's good.

Alan (*laughs*)   Nobody is trying to spite anyone here, okay? He could have called a cab, couldn't he? (*Rising.*) I'll phone him if you like. Tell him I have them.

Nicola (*appalled*)   And what would you say . . . that it dawned on you now? (*To the others.*) I'm out of order, I'm sorry. I know you've other things to discuss.

She gets up from the table. She goes and sits on the balcony. She picks up the cigarettes beside the plinth. She lights up. **Alan** *watches her, concerned.*

Stephen   Heard you had a bit of a calamity in that bar last weekend, Alan.

Alan   What? Yeah, we did. Sunday night, we were flooded. Why do you ask?

Stephen   Arcadia, yes?

Alan   That's the name of the place. I've only been there a few months, Stephen. (*Rising.*) Nicola, sweet. I picked them up, I forgot. I picked them up, I put them in my pocket . . .

Stephen   Seems there was significant water damage around those environs. A lot of shops boarded up. It was a catastrophe, wasn't it?

Alan   Yeah, well, what can you do, Stephen? Weather is weather. (*Exasperated.*) Sit down with us, Nicola. Your dinner's getting cold. (*Laughs.*) Seriously, folks. She's got the wrong end of the stick here . . .

Stephen   So, what's the clientele like, then? In Arcadia?

Amy (*urgent*)   Stephen.

Alan *turns to* **Amy**. *He sighs.*

Alan (*laughs, in wonder*)   I almost forgot you were here! (*Beat, sombre.*) Now, I remember. (*To* **Stephen**.) You were saying . . . ?

Stephen (*shrugs*)   Oh, well, it's not a major thing, really. I have an interest, that's all. The clientele in bars, the kind of people, you see, who chose one place over another. (*Laughs.*) Personally, I put it down mainly to music. Music, the décor. Well, all of those touches, they create an ambience. The bar can be seen as a social barometer. An institution, you see? (*Beat.*) No, the reason, my friends, for my specific enquiry, is that I've yet to have the pleasure of paying you a visit. Now, I dropped down there this morning, I was doing my rounds, but . . .

Amy   You were there? There, as well?

Stephen   The man *wasn't in* – will you please let me finish, petal? I went in, had a look-see. Curiosity, you know, since I'd just met you yesterday. Now, no problem, no problem, I didn't quite meet the dress code. But as I've said . . . if you'll indulge my theory. (*Beat.*) The spare wooden flooring. The white lights, the big windows. It's a nice crowd, then, is it? A young crowd, convivial?

Alan *is bewildered. He looks to* **Amy** *for help. She refuses to meet his eye.*

Nicola *stubs her cigarette out. She gets up, she comes in, she addresses the table.*

Nicola   Okay, you people, you know, you need to knuckle right down to it. You need to say what's on your mind, because inevitably otherwise . . . (*Beat.*) Well, when certain people avoid things, emotions can . . . fester. (*Pointing to* **Alan**.) Him. Him there. (*Laughs.*) I don't care who knows it, because it's adolescent now, isn't it? Richard and I, we used to *go out*. And him. He can't take it!

Stephen *and* **Nicola**'s *eyes meet accidentally.* **Nicola** *bursts into laughter, suddenly aware of this shambolic sight. The spirit of madness has come to the table –* **Stephen** *and* **Nicola** *are drunk,* **Amy** *is stoned.* **Alan** *stares open-mouthed as order seems to collapse.*

Stephen *reaches for the wine. He notices* **Alan**'s *puzzlement.*

Alan   Look, Nicola, at least I told you the truth. Did you ever think about that, did you? I could have lied to you, couldn't I? I could have said there was someone else. I wasn't doing it to spite him . . . (*With a look to* **Stephen** *and* **Amy**.) This wasn't exactly as I'd hoped tonight would work out, you know.

Stephen (*pouring* **Alan** *wine*)   It's a malaise.

Alan   What?

Stephen   It's a malaise is what it is; a malaise, a malaise.

Alan (*to* **Amy**)   And what's he talking about now, huh?

Stephen (*rising*)   The girl's got a point, of course. (*Sadly amused.*) Oh, this splenetic city, with its heart wrapped in ice . . . (*Cheerfully to* **Alan**, *regarding* **Amy**.) Play catch-up. Knuckle down, man. I'll absent myself: point me to the commode . . .

He gets up. Both **Alan** *and* **Amy** *look at him in panic.*

Stephen *lumbers off. He notices* **Nicola** *sitting alone. He goes to her.*

Stephen   Now, let's get one thing straight, cupcake. The great God of wine, he's an innocent here. He's *largely* an innocent, and I've done the rounds, miss. So, I don't want you berating yourself about having too much to drink. You're an angel, come hither. You are a lovely girl. (*Moving closer to her, sotto voce.*) You're in on it, right? Alan's heard a rumour?

Nicola *nods nervously. She turns away.*

Stephen (*grandly, to the others*)   And what is one to surmise? This . . . splenetic new city, the . . . metamorphosis. (*Amused now.*) Can you imagine the scene? The Great God Bacchus: god of wine and our revels. Master of illusion. Imagine, if you will, the Great God Dionysus, he looks down on our homestead – he observes the many citizens, spewing bile, spitting blood. He thinks to himself, 'Curious, curious!' So, right there and then, in the middle of a storm, he sets out on a quest – leapfrogging into the body of a mortal that falls. He enters the metropolis, he has a bit of a look-see. (*Sotto voce, to* **Nicola**.) What has he heard, love? What's the take on this . . . chaos?

Nicola (*coolly*)   Stephen.

Stephen   Yes?

Nicola   Back off.

Alan *turns away from* **Amy**. *He is distracted by* **Stephen**.

Amy (*losing her cool*)   Look, don't mind him, don't mind him. He's obsessed with the pubs, Alan. He's obsessed with the idea that there's some kind of malaise, but he'll keep swearing at you until he's blue in the face that the drink's not problem . . . (*A little panicked.*) Is there something you've been wanting to ask me? Because, as I've said, this sets a precedent . . .

Stephen   In point of fact, I was kicked in the head today.

Amy   He wasn't kicked in the head. Listen to me, would you?

Stephen   A feral young fellow chose to confront me. (*Turning to* **Nicola**.) Loaded, it appeared, but feral nonetheless. (*Laughs.*)

I mean, let's just face it, they're all beating the shit out of each other. They're beating the shit out of each other, the parents, the kids. Grown professional men are beating the shit out of each other. They're running amok, flailing about the shop. But naturally, eh? Naturally, the government . . .

Amy (*suddenly hugely angry, turning to* **Stephen**)   And what's that about? What's that about? I think you know full well what we're on about, don't you? Whose side are you on? Are you *trying* to antagonise me?

Alan (*firmly*)   Amy. Enough.

Amy (*alarmed*)   What?

Stephen *looks at them a moment. He seems satisfied. He goes off.*

Amy (*to* **Alan**)   So, all right, you win! I got fired from the Institute. The Advanced Institution for Educational Enrichment. I got fired – it's outrageous . . . I was subbing for someone, I'd been there six weeks. (*Beat.*) So, I told a white lie. Mammy knows, you can tell her . . .

Alan *just looks at her.*

Amy   Look, you couldn't possibly imagine what it was like there, all right? It's a summer school, isn't it? Oh, it's very prestigious. Mostly, it seems, they're kids who want to skip university and get out in the real world. I was apparently supposed to help them with their CVs. (*Laughs.*) Laugh? Oh, we did. (*Sighs.*) Not that, to be fair, it was entirely my fault. My first day on the job I had a chair lobbed straight at me. They'd never sit still, and their phones, and their iPods . . . (*Laughs.*) They weren't only yobs, see? Most of them were . . . rich!

Alan   So, what did you . . . do? To get fired, I mean?

Amy (*sigh: she can't bear to tell him*)   It's a . . . teacup!

Alan   And she thinks I'm the one having a quarter-life crisis!

He gets up.

Nicola (*angry*)   Oh, you're impossible! Get over yourselves, would you? The kid is Jonathan's nephew!

Amy   Jonathan? Who's *Jonathan*?

Nicola (*laughs*)   Oh, you can't possibly tell me you don't know who he is. Jonathan Gray and Richard Carlisle! That award-winning partnership, they own a whole string of bars. *Allegedly*, Amy, you roughed up some kid pretty bad, right? Some kid in that school . . . the Advanced Institution. Now, sweetie, I'm sorry, I'm not even *involved* here, but it's murder . . . the pair of you, and now it seems Alan's taken to *thieving*. Jonathan Gray and Richard Carlisle, they're his bosses, aren't they? (*Sighs.*) The kid is Jonathan's *nephew*, he works down the bar sometimes. He's Jonathan's nephew, Alan *knows* him, you get it? (*Sighs.*) This pussyfooting around . . .

Stephen *comes on. He stares at the ivy. The extent of his drunkenness is now apparent. He takes a silver hip-flask from his pocket. He uncaps it, takes a drink.*

Amy   Stephen.

Stephen   Yes?

Amy   We're leaving. (*She goes.*)

Stephen (*shrugs*)   Well, as Amy goes, so goes my nation. (*He hesitates.*) June 21st. That mean anything to you, eh?

Amy (*off*)   Stephen!

Stephen *goes off.*

Nicola (*exasperated*)   Don't even look at me. We've officially got . . . problems!

Act Two

Darkness. A neon sign fizzes into life: it reads 'Arcadia'.

Lights up. The set appears to have 'revolved' slightly – the furniture has been pushed to new positions. We're in the back room of a bar now. The balcony area has become a storage area for a display shelf, holding bottles. Most of the other furniture remains the same. The only natural light source is presumed to come from a skylight above. It is the next day. Early afternoon.

*We discover **Scott**. He is sixteen. He speaks into a mobile phone as he searches the room for something, removing cushions from the couch, peering in corners, etc.*

Scott (*to phone*)   Wanker! You wanker. No, I already did that, I came in to check, I . . . (*Anxious.*) There's only three days left here, you know, we can't put this off, okay? There's only so much time . . . (*Indignant.*) Down? You go down there. Well, you're going *to have to* 'breach the perimeter'. Make something up, Jeff! Scale the fence if you have to.

He stops in mid-track. He realises the magnitude of his situation. He is struck by a sudden tremor.

Ah, you mother . . . ! (*He looks about. He's almost spinning. To phone.*) Listen, all right, I'll have one last look downstairs. (*Angry.*) I am pretty damn sure you went down there, Jeffrey. What do you mean, for what? To take a piss, are you touched? Don't whine at me like that . . . !

A bell rings.

(*Anxiously.*) Crap. Someone's coming. Look, change of plan, hold off on the breaching until you hear from me, okay? I'm just after having a really screwed-up idea . . .

He snaps his phone shut. A door 'opens'. More light. A figure lurks, indistinct, the arrangement of light and dark obscuring the presence.

Emm, if you're just gonna stand there – I can see you, you know.

The lights equalise. They reveal **Alan***, a hand at a light-switch. Over his shoulder he carries a suit, encased in a protective bag.*

Scott   Alan?

Alan (*surprised*)   Scott.

Scott   You spooked me out a bit, dog! Dig the stealthy approach?

Alan *goes to the table. He looks slowly around the room . . . noticing one of the cushions from the couch on the floor, some other mild disarray.*

Scott   Problem?

Alan   A problem, Scott? Now, where shall we begin? First of all, see, the front door was open. Coming in a close second, there's your actual presence.

Scott (*laughs, sincerely, at the absurdity*)   You look rattled to me. Think I was *robbing* the place?

Alan (*laughs*)   Now, Scott, come on . . . we're all friends here, right?

Scott   I wasn't robbing the place. You think I'm some kind of chav? (*Friendly now.*) What has you down here and where are all the Polish girls anyway?

Alan   It's a Saturday, Scott. We open at five.

He just looks at **Scott***. He picks up the cushion. He puts it in its place.*

Scott   Tak, tak, tak, tak. I arrived, Mr Simms, via the front door. I let myself in . . . (*Fumbling in his pocket for keys.*) Check it out, dude, observe. (*He produces an unremarkable bunch of keys.*) They're Jonathan's keys. They're Jonathan's keys, he gave them to me, what with him being at that fat-camp in Karlovy Vari. He remarked to me – what I mean is *he heard*, he'd heard about the flood. And he said to me I should swing by, like, the weekend. Clean the windows and that, get the place looking spruce.

Alan   Clean the windows?

Scott   He said he'd slip me a ton. I mean, come on, I have debts!

Alan *looks about. He's not entirely convinced but seems presently satisfied.*

Scott   Excellent, so, we're all in agreement. I'll just drop in downstairs now, if that's book by you. Find a basin, some rags . . .

He begins to walk away. **Alan** *looks at him, appalled.*

Scott   What's the kim?

Alan   Six days now, is it? Six days since the . . . beating?

Scott   And?

Alan   Well, excuse me for saying so, but you look . . . fit and well to me.

Scott *looks at him a moment. And then, bored, he pulls up his T-shirt to reveal a patchwork of ugly purple bruises all over his back.*

Alan *(appalled)*   Forgive me, I . . . that just came out like that.

Scott *(shrugs)*   That's okay, boss. Bygones, you know. It looks worse than it feels, I reckon. *(Shrugs.)* I'm on a truckload of a lot of painkillers: something feels torn here. *(Sudden laughter.)* Hey, but life's wild.

Alan   You know she's my . . . sister, right?

Scott   That's very impressive. I didn't think you'd have the muscle.

Alan *(looks at him, embarrassed)*   Anyway, as I said . . . *(Scowls.)* Then get to work, get your basin.

He pulls down the zip on his bag. He removes a grey suit. He hangs it up. **Scott** *watches him a moment, he shrugs, turns to go.* **Alan** *turns back to him.*

Alan   Okay, then, great: we're all friends here. I'm going to be straight with you, yeah? I don't want to seem rude, or insensitive, or anything. I don't want to short-change the . . . trauma you've . . . *(Beat.)* I wasn't expecting you. I wasn't prepared. *(Irritated.)* Besides, I should have been told that you had keys to the building, Scott.

Scott   Take it up with the Man, man.

Alan   I didn't exactly sleep too soundly last night, either. If you must know, I . . . (*Trying for a joke, not realising the implication.*) Well, it seems around here lately, people are always misplacing things . . .

Scott *looks at him, attentive. Misplacing what?*

Alan (*innocently*)   Did I say something? What?

Scott *doesn't move.*

Alan   She's my sister, you know. She did that? *How?*

Scott (*slowly*)   You didn't . . . find anything, did you?

Alan   Find anything? What d'you mean, did I find anything?

Scott   Did you find anything yesterday? When you opened back up?

Alan   I'm not talking about yesterday. I'm talking about my sister.

Scott *looks at him anxiously.* **Alan** *notices* **Scott***'s urgency.*

Alan (*cautiously*)   *Richard* sent you here? To get something for him?

They look at one another.

Scott   Look, I don't know squat about Richard looking for anything. If Richard . . . he happened . . . well, that's irrelevant, isn't it? I just asked you, that's all, if you'd happened to find something. Because *you* said, you . . .

Alan (*relieved*)   Richard didn't send you?

Scott   No!

He scowls. He has a thought. He looks about. He turns back to **Alan***.*

You . . . ?

Alan   Yes?

Scott   Nothing.

Alan *looks at* **Scott** *a moment, confused.*

Alan   Okay, I've apologised twice now if I was rude to you, Scott. If you really must know, I feel slightly . . . sickened. She and I, we're not close. (*Still shocked by the memory of* **Scott**'s *bruises.*) She did that to you?

Scott   What gave you the impression that Richard sent me down here?

Alan (*ignoring the question*)   I mean, this isn't exactly what I'd call a 'teacup' now, is it? (*Beat.*) She called it a teacup. That is her way, Scott. (*Beat.*) Look, between you and me now. You don't kid around with allegations like that. Between you and me, if there's something else going on here – well, there's still time, you know, no one has to suffer. We all make mistakes. You want to tell me why she hasn't heard from the police yet?

Scott *just looks at him.*

Alan   I would think, with respect, in a situation like this, Scott –

Scott   Maybe, the police, they've already charged her. Maybe, you know, she didn't tell you they had!

Alan *considers this a moment. It's a possibility.*

Scott *looks at* **Alan** *again. He's sizing him up.*

Alan   Look, I'm trying to stay neutral here. What do you want me to say to you?

Scott   I'll go get that basin.

He goes off.

Alan (*calling after him*)   It's just not sitting too well with me that no one said you were working. I'll have to call Jonathan. Just to check up, you know.

He heaves a sigh. He takes out the set of keys he had earlier.

Close call. (*He picks up the phone. He dials. He tosses the keys in the air. To phone.*) Yeah, Nicola. Yeah, it's me. I know that we're not officially talking and that, but this is your voicemail and I'm not sure if that qualifies. About last night, I . . . (*Sighs.*) Well, there's

nothing else I can say that I didn't say last night. It wasn't a
question of *thieving*, okay? It's just, Richard made that comment
yesterday, and I simply, I . . . (*Beat.*) Okay, so maybe it's true,
I wanted to spite him. That doesn't mean it's about you sleeping
with him, Nicola. It was stupid and petty, adolescent behaviour
and I'm sorting that problem out, right now as we speak, yeah?
(*Gravely.*) The kid is here now. That's a dark sight. (*Plaintive.*)
Anyhow, call me back when you're free. Let's be mature about
this. (*He hangs up.*) Stupid. And petty. Adolescent behaviour.

He drops the keys to the floor. He kicks them under the couch.

No harm done then, so. Richard can find them himself.

Scott *comes on, empty-handed.* **Alan** *looks at him.*

Scott   What?

Alan   Your basin?

Scott   I couldn't find one.

Alan   Well, I'm pretty damn sure there's a bucket at least.
(*Laughs.*) Don't you want to get paid? I mean, that's why you're
here, right?

Scott   Climbing those stairs. It's took the wind out of me.
(*Slyly.*) I'll just sit down for a few minutes if that's book by you.
I'll go back, get the bucket.

He doesn't move. He stares at **Alan** *again.* **Alan** *is bewildered.*

Alan   What? Will you relax? Why do you keep *looking* at me
like that?

Scott   No reason.

Alan   I would think, with respect, that there must be
something. There must be some reason . . . (*Beat.*) You think . . .
let me see – you think I don't believe you? You think *I think*
you're lying? That someone else . . . beat you up?

Scott   I couldn't give a fart in the breeze about what you
think about that, champ.

Alan   You couldn't?

Scott   No disrespect, of course. (*Slyly.*) We all know you're the boss.

Alan (*exasperated*)   Get your bucket . . .

Scott   I thought I already said: I need to rest for five minutes. (*Stressed out.*) You think you're the only one with problems? (*Laughs, with disdain.*) What, 'cause you're running a bar? No disrespect, dog. It's not like you own the place, is it?

Alan (*suitably chastised*)   I'm well aware of that fact, Scott.

Scott (*laughs*)   Now, Jonathan, *Richard*. (*Beat.*) Richard's been on TV. You seen that car he drives, have you? Have you seen his *honey* . . . ? (*Laughs.*) He brought myself and the guys once, he took us to Lotus. Have you been to Lotus? Well, the *women* there, man . . . (*Beat.*) Getting a car next month, dog. An old Civic to start with; of course, I'll have to pimp it up. (*Beat.*) I won't be a factotum. Like, this is the sum total?

Alan (*disguising humiliation*)   You done now?

Scott   Done? (*Laughs.*) Ah now, come on, there's no need to get paranoid. How old are you, thirty? I see you in here. I see those sidelong glances. Those Polish girls, boss. I bet they think you're the bee's knees.

Alan   Well, when you grow up a bit, Scott . . .

Scott (*amused*)   A lecture.

Alan   Well, you'll realise there's a bit more to life than . . . (*Indignant.*) I've been to Lotus. You think I haven't been there? (*Irritated.*) You're still a kid, you know. I have some life experience.

Scott   I'm a kid?

Alan   You're sixteen.

Scott   And if Richard sees fit to let me and the guys have a drink now and then, just exactly what business is that of yours anyway? You're not too crazy about Richard, that's what I reckon, see? Is that because he's a success? Is that the reason now, champ, that you clearly resent of one this country's richest – ?

Alan (*enraged*)   Tell me what happened with Amy!

Scott   Oh. Touched a nerve.

Alan (*grimly*)   Stephen said that on Monday, your class had been cancelled.

Scott   And who's he? Her lawyer?

Alan   Just answer the question! (*Beat.*) Well, the story as I heard is that Amy cancelled a class. You turned up at the classroom in a bit of a stink. She was in the staff room alone –

Scott   She was smoking a spliff, man!

Alan (*sighs*)   Well, yes, so I hear. Amy has problems, I'm not excusing that. (*Sighs.*) Amy made a few comments about your negative attitude, and suggested to you that you use the free time to catch up on your studies . . . (*Slowly.*) You made a passing remark about what she was wearing . . .

Scott (*shrugs*)   The woman dresses like a Bosnian.

Alan   And then?

Scott   And then she . . . hit me.

Alan   Well, that's not what she says happened, is it? She says that she fainted.

Scott (*shrugs*)   So?

Silence. **Alan** *looks at* **Scott** *more closely.*

Scott (*frustrated*)   Look, she wigged out on me, all right? She *overloaded* or something . . . (*Laughs.*) Now, me and the guys, we can be a handful, but there's no call for that, that's majorly unacceptable. So, she had her big *frisson*, she went for the kill, man. And then she kicked me a few times – some girls these days do that. (*Beat.*) Accept it, my friend, the woman's a basket case. (*He looks at* **Alan** *a moment.*) What gave you the impression that Richard sent me down here today, anyway?

Alan   Yourself and 'the guys', maybe you have a scuffle. Someone gets . . . hurt . . . Scott, do you hear what I'm saying? (*Beat.*) You know what else I'm thinking? Why would a kid in your . . . damaged condition be volunteering to wash those windows anyway? You want to answer me that, do you? Exactly what's going on here?

They look at one another. Both are quivering with rage.

A thump as something hits the skylight from above. It casts a shadow across the floor.

Scott (*dazed*)   What was that?

Alan (*looking up, unmoving*)   It's a bird.

Scott (*bored*)   Yeah, well, that's ace. (*Beat.*) Look, I've got to make a call. (*He checks his pockets.*) Left the phone downstairs, typical.

He walks away. He turns back.

I've got a hunch about you, yeah?

He goes off.

Alan *curses silently. He looks up at the skylight. He makes a decision. He picks up the phone.*

Alan   Jonathan's away. (*To phone.*) Richard. Hello, Richard, it's Alan Simms here. (*Trying to remain calm.*) I hope you are . . . well. Saturday, at eleven. Look, when you get this message, can you call me at the bar, please? It's just that I . . . (*Beat.*) Look, well, please call. I need to speak to you personally. (*Scowls.*) I don't really know how you're going to feel about this, Richard, but I think you and I, we need to talk about Scott. I know that you might find the subject distasteful. Look, can you tell me if Scott was supposed to clean the windows today? I know it sounds trivial . . . (*Beat.*) Look, just call me here when you get a minute.

He hangs up the phone.

A bell rings.

Voice (*off*)   Hello?

Alan   Come on in.

Voice (*off*)   Anyone home, then? Any life in the house?

Alan   We're closed until five. Can't you read the sign?

Stephen *comes on, in shadow.*

Alan   You seem to be making a habit of coming in uninvited, Stephen.

Stephen *steps curiously into the room. He is wearing a suit identical to the one hanging. He seems rejuvenated.*

Stephen   *Et in arcadia ego.*

Alan   Not to be rude, but you might have called first, maybe.

Stephen (*looking about*)   The name, one supposes, is some kind of ironic twist. The pastoral theme. A bough in the shade. The atmosphere, I imagine, is anything but.

Alan   The name was Jonathan's concept.

Stephen   And if the establishment was *yours*, sir, what would you call it? We're presuming, of course, you have a little ambition. (*Wandering about.*) You notice how these places all have a similar moniker? A womb. Or a shield. A delicate flower. It's almost as if the drinking's beside the point.

Alan   The kid is downstairs, you know.

Stephen   He is? (*Amused, noticing the dead bird.*) Is that a . . . thrush?

Alan   I've been thinking, you know, about what you were saying last night. That kid you met in the pub? Well, it's possible, isn't it, that he and Scott are acquainted. It's certainly worth pursuing . . . and Scott, well, we *spoke* and . . . (*Overwhelmed.*) Now, I've seen the bruises, but . . . (*Sighs.*) Look, you can tell Amy for me that I believe her, okay? You can tell her for sure . . . I don't think she did it.

Stephen *looks at him a moment. He's pleased.*

Stephen (*cheerfully*)   Looks like we've got the same suit, hey?

Amy *comes on. She looks like death. She is wearing sunglasses.*

Alan (*a refusal to admit her*)   Amy!

Stephen   Thought we'd advanced a cubit.

Alan *stops short, appalled by her appearance.*

Amy (*fiercely*)   What?

Alan   Your timing's atrocious! The kid's on his way up!

Stephen (*to* **Amy**)   There's a dead thrush up there. Or a sparrow.

Enter **Scott**, *speaking into his mobile phone.*

Scott   What I'm saying to you, Jeffrey, is he's got a plug up his butt. (*Very low, to the phone.*) I can't. He's right here. No, I can't do that, Jeffrey, I can't simply ask . . . (*Beat.*) Look, just shut up. Let me make a call.

He snaps his phone shut. **Stephen** *puts an arm around* **Amy***'s shoulder.*

Alan   Now, with respect for the place, I'd like if everyone stays calm.

Scott *turns to go. He doesn't seem to recognise* **Amy**.

Alan   Scott, this is Stephen. (*Heavily.*) And Amy.

Scott (*with disdain*)   Like, what, you're a Goth now?

He goes off.

Amy (*furious*)   I could kill him!

Stephen   Death is wasted on the young.

Amy   You see what I have to contend with? Has it dawned on you yet?

Alan   You're the one who stormed out last night.

Amy   And you summoned me there under false pretences! You made me stew all that time. Pretending you wanted to be friends with me!

Alan   Well, maybe if you'd been just a little bit more forthcoming . . . (*Scowls.*) I hadn't even got to the stage of forming an opinion. (*Sighs.*) Look, Stephen, I . . . will you excuse us a minute?

Stephen   Gladly.

He makes to go off. He hesitates.

Come to think of it, I . . .

Alan   Yes?

Stephen   No matter, no matter. Amy will fill you in.

He goes off.

Alan (*laughs*)   Well. You know how to pick them, I'll say that much for you, anyway. (*Awkwardly.*) That's not the same suit at all, Amy? This is a Patrick Frame suit. Have you any idea what it cost me?

A bell rings.

(*Hollow.*) I don't believe that you did it. I'm sure that Mam wouldn't either. The fact that we're, what . . . we're estranged, is that it? I believe you, all right? What is it you want from me?

Silence.

Here is the situation as I see it, yes? I think that it's time you took some legal advice. I think, even though, as I perhaps half-suspected, even though I'm pretty sure there's something . . . ill going on here, I don't think the kid's going to back down, okay? I don't have a clue why he thought to blame you for it. Maybe because you fainted, you're an easy target. Maybe he didn't like your attitude, that's all. (*Beat.*) But if your strategy is simply to stick your head in the sand . . .

Amy   The school said they're looking for some security tape!

Alan   And, you see? Exactly!

Amy   What do you mean exactly?

Alan   When you were Scott's age, you used to go *missing*. There's a problem at home, you just vanished, didn't you? So, you'd head for the hills, rather than confront it. I can relate to that, sort of. (*Laughs, grimly.*) But if you think that these kids . . . well, they're a different breed to us, aren't they? They are completely fearless. It's like a head-on collision. And I am

suggesting to you, you take some legal advice, because if a kid
like that, Amy, he decides to sink you, well, you can take it
from me, he'll find a way and a means. Slip security fifty, and
then there's no tape. I'm not saying that happened. But it's
possible, isn't it? And, if you're not careful, you're going to
find yourself in a situation where it's your word against his,
Amy. Now, when they bring up your history of emotional . . .
problems . . . and factor-in the fact that the kid saw you
smoking a joint in there –

Amy (*frustrated*)   I had my head out the window! I wasn't
even teaching that day!

Alan   I'm trying to help you here, woman! Can't you . . .
what . . . can't you stop?

Amy (*quietly*)   You've changed your tune.

Alan   So, maybe I have. But don't you go and presume that
we're singing the same song, all right?

Amy *takes off the shades. She looks at* **Alan***, vaguely amused.*

Amy   You want to know something?

Alan   I'm sure you're going to tell me.

Amy   You want to know why I think you and I never got
on, Alan? You want me to explain this suspicion . . . this . . .
distance? (*Shrugs.*) There was a measure of . . . warmth before
I turned sixteen. There was at least a small measure, after all,
we were kids, right? (*Sadly.*) But as I . . . matured, I began to
look at you differently. Now I know they say girls, they mature
before boys, but I can't help but think it was more serious than
that. I became slowly convinced that you had no code.

Alan (*laughs*)   A *code*? Are you kidding me?

Amy (*increasingly assured*)   Don't be fatuous, please. I am
opening up here. (*Scowls.*) You were . . . dull. You were dull.
You were dull, dull, dull, dull. You never had any code that
I could recognise anyway. You just went with the flow. The
rising tide, you might say. (*Scowls.*) You had posters of sports
cars draped all over your bedroom. You were so glibly, so

blindly, so *seduced* by extravagance . . . (*Beat.*) I can't blame you
for that; we all know the forces at work here. But it's meant
I can't trust you. And now, I ask your forgiveness.

She looks at him a moment. He's thrown by the admission.

Alan   . . . Forgiveness?

Amy   I also apologise for the dig about Gustav Klimt.

Alan   Now you ask my *forgiveness*? After that *tirade*? (*Laughs.*)
You think my heart's wrapped in ice – I'm trying to help you
here, aren't I? Is it because I work? The people I call my
friends? (*Irritated.*) I mean, do you think that you're waving the
working-class banner here? You're somehow more authentic?

Amy   It's not like we were brought up on a council estate, is it?

Alan   No, it isn't!

Amy (*sighs*)   I get depressed. I'm depressive.

Alan (*slowly*)   And . . . ?

Amy   So, then all this *rising above*, it's . . . (*Sighs.*) Those of us
who can't manage . . . well, we're a waste of space, aren't we?
Oh, they'll deny it. They'll deny it to the hilt with their . . .
awareness campaigns, but secretly, Alan, we all know it's a
moral issue. (*Beat.*) Something happened to me that day in the
classroom. I mean, *before.* I came in that day and I cancelled
my class. I knew I wasn't cut out for it. Now, one job, that's no
biggie – there are plenty of people who aren't cut out for
teaching. But there's been *nothing* thus far that I've been cut
out for, okay? (*Laughs.*) I'm thirty-eight years old! (*Laughs.*)
Thirty-five's the new twenty. That's what the press office says.
And that would make me still young, but . . . (*Shrugs.*) I mean,
since we're speaking our minds . . . A few days before I'd
reached a big decision. I had decided that I'd finally come off
the pills, see? Now, as regards that, there are *side-effects*, I . . .
(*Sighs.*) I remember quite clearly Scott made that remark.
I remember that look, so aloof, so self-righteous . . . (*Laughs.*)
I woke up on the floor. (*Beat.*) The blacking out, well, that's
chemical, isn't it . . . neurological, even . . . (*Beat.*) Look, we all

know the forces at work here, the malaise gets turned inwards. You've got no career, no status, no *substance*. You're still renting a flat, people think there's something wrong with you. The clothes on your back. After a while, you start to think that something's wrong, too. (*Beat.*) You think I'm finding this easy?

Silence.

Alan (*awkwardly, laughs*)   Look, it's not exactly like I'm an investment banker or something. We're renting as well, Amy. Nicola's not what you'd call flush.

Amy (*sincere, plaintive*)   I *know* that. I *see* that. I'm saying we wipe the slate clean, okay? We take . . . ownership.

Alan *looks at her a moment. He seems at least partially convinced.*

Alan   Okay.

Amy   You really want to help me?

Alan   Well, how about we just say I had a hunch about those kids, all right?

Amy (*embarrassed*)   You want to hug?

Alan *looks at her a moment. He is embarrassed. He doesn't move.*

Amy   I mean, can't you see it? This . . . sadness about us?

Alan *looks at her a moment. He laughs.*

Alan   I'm not the one who's unhappy here!

Amy   Did I say that you were?

Alan   I am trying to *help* you. I'm trying to figure this out. Don't you start in on my quarter-life crisis because I . . . (*He sighs, he looks about.*) I kind of get the impression Scott was here for a reason. I kind of got the impression he was *looking* for something.

Amy   Probably looking for those keys that you pinched off your boss, huh? Which we're all glad to see have been faithfully returned to him.

Alan   What?

Amy (*amused*)   You want to explain that one, anyway? What were you doing, acting out?

Alan   What do you mean, 'They've been faithfully returned to him'?

Amy   The keys. Richard has them.

Alan   I don't think so.

Amy   Well, he must have, you know, because we saw Richard not an hour ago. (*Shrugs.*) I'd know that face. I saw him on the TV once. (*Shrugs.*) Stephen took me to Melon, it's an organic juice bar. It was a gesture, you see, but I'll explain that later. As we were lumbering in through those revolving doors, there was the bonny boy, revolving out. There was a pretty stick-insect with about four thousand shopping bags clinging to his arm. They jumped into the car, and pulled away from the kerb. The whole display, to be honest, was kind of debauched.

Alan *is shocked. He looks over to the couch. A thought strikes him.*

Alan   Richard's still driving, then?

He goes over to the couch. He kicks it back.

Amy   What? What's the matter?

Alan *bends down. He picks up the keys.*

Alan   You see, I just *presumed* they were Richard's keys. I just decided that because Richard seemed frantic, and I'd found a set of keys behind one of the loos, right? Now, it's possible, of course, he has a replacement set. Or maybe, you know, he contacted the . . . dealership, but that's pretty doubtful. I don't think they're his. Maybe, then, Richard – he was looking for something else entirely . . . and maybe Scott, he . . .

He looks at the keys. He is deep in thought. He tosses them in the air.

A bell rings.

Stephen.

He pockets the keys.

Amy (*urgent*)   Look, he's an alcoholic, okay?

Alan What?

Amy Stephen. He's an alcoholic, he wants you to know, that's all. (*Urgent.*) I think he's awfully guilty. Because I've enabled him, okay? He thinks that my . . . problems, well, I think he partly blames himself for them. (*Sighs.*) Stephen and I, we've struck a bargain, Alan. He'll jack in the booze, for good this time, he means it. And me? (*Sighs.*) I'm not saying for a moment I'll be sweetness and light. (*Laughs.*) Stephen thinks it's unnatural when families are estranged, Alan. Maybe it's a blessing that this whole mess has happened.

They look at each other a moment. **Amy** *smiles.*

Stephen *comes on, followed by* **Scott**.

Stephen (*to* **Scott**) Wine had a mystery. Wine – and beer, too, lad: now, let's not get elitist. Delirium was . . . sacred. Via the Bacchic mysteries, the soul – it took flight . . . (*Beat.*) The nigredo, if briefly, was washed away: the banished chthonic and pure white albeda, they merged into one, hmmm? That was the true bacchanal. It wasn't some quest for . . . stupefaction. Rather a search for *oneself*, yes? And those that met madness, along the route? Well, they had either refused to worship, or were worshipping the wrong way. (*Lost for words.*) What kind of music do you like, then?

He notices **Alan** *and* **Amy**, *staring at him.*

Stephen Gentlemen, ladies.

Alan (*regarding* **Scott**) And would you look who's come back, huh?

Amy (*shrugs, embarrassed*) Stephen has a way with these people.

Alan (*lost*) Stephen . . . ?

Scott *looks about the room, nervously. He's expecting* **Stephen** *to speak.*

Stephen Scott has all but admitted he knows my young friend from The Wren.

Scott (*outraged*) Yo, I never said that!

Stephen   Do you want our assistance, boy, or do you not? (*Laughs. To the others.*) I gripped our friend by both arms. (*Gripping* **Scott**.) Like this, do you see? I said to the boy, 'Child, I think you need our assistance.' I looked him straight in the eye. Desperation, correct? That same hunted look that I saw last night. Friends, we all guessed that. Conspirators, at least. June 21st, eh? My assailant's name is Jeff Boston.

Scott   Let me go.

Amy   Stephen. Let him go. You're hurting his arm.

Scott (*struggling*)   Anybody ever tell you you're a knob jockey?

Stephen (*still holding on, amused, to the others*)   I mentioned the date: June 21st. Told him, perhaps, I could help him out.

Amy (*urgent*)   Stephen!

Stephen (*releasing* **Scott**)   Very well.

Alan *produces the keys. He holds them up.*

Alan   Know anything about these, huh?

Scott *reaches for the keys.*

Alan   Oh, no! I don't think so. Not at least until we get some answers, okay?

Stephen (*to* **Amy**)   You want to fill me in here?

Alan   Who gave you those bruises? Are you protecting somebody? (*Regarding keys.*) What's this we all hear about June 21st and why do you seem to want these so badly?

Alan *and* **Stephen** *move in on* **Scott**.

Scott *is struck by a tremor.*

Stephen   Interesting. Tremors.

Scott   Now, you lot keep back! Keep back or I'll . . . !

Panicked, he takes a small metal object from his pocket. He presses a switch. A blade shoots out. He waves it about.

(*Increasingly hysterical, backing away.*) Don't think for a minute I'm afraid to use this. (*Enraged.*) Oh, you mother, I swear!

He trips and falls. The weapon skids out of reach. **Scott** *scrambles to his feet. He shudders again. He goes off.*

Alan *puts the keys on the table.*

Alan (*grimly*)   I think we can safely say that's a development, isn't it?

A bell rings.

(*To* **Amy**.) Don't you think for a second we're going to let this pass . . . I think this already proves . . . Well, it clearly proves something. The kid's going to retract what he said about you, all right?

Amy   Should we call the police?

Alan   We'll see about that. We'll see about that just as soon as we . . . (*Beat.*) I've always known there's something ill going on here. Now, I don't know to what extent Richard is aware of all this, but I can tell you for certain I'm not standing by. (*Beat.*) Nicola's not going to like it. She won't like it at all. But this has nothing to do with the fact they went out, so . . . (*Wry.*) looks like we're on the same side?

He scowls. He goes to the phone and picks it up.

Amy (*awkwardly, to* **Stephen**)   And what are you looking so pleased about?

Alan (*to phone*)   Yes, hello Richard. It's Alan Simms again. (*Very firm.*) I would appreciate it if you phone me *immediately*. I'm pretty sure that Scott's in some kind of . . . trouble.

He slams the phone down. He looks up at the skylight.

Stephen   Well, all this seems to have gone swimmingly. How about we repair . . . the ginger ale is on me!

Blackout. The neon sign burns in the darkness.

Act Three

Birdsong.

The bar. The set has revolved again, revealing the scene from a different angle. The following morning, about 11 a.m. The aftershock of an evening's boozing: a number of empty bottles, glasses and plates of food are scattered about the room. Pale morning sun from the skylight above: much of the set is shrouded in darkness. The neon sign is unlit.

Alan, *alone. He is sitting behind the table, the telephone lodged in the crook of his neck. He is rolling a joint. He is wearing the suit that was previously hanging: he's looking pretty dishevelled, however. On the table in front of him is an open bottle of wine, a glass and an ash-tray. Elsewhere lie a megaphone and a stack of old newspapers.*

Alan (*to phone*)   No, I didn't. Yes, I did. Yes. Yes. (*Sighs.*) That's fair enough, Amy, I know you're upset, but . . . (*Irritated.*) No, I couldn't reach Jonathan. Well, he's on a health farm now, isn't he? (*Sighs.*) I know. I know. Well, no, I haven't done that either, I wanted to sleep on it, okay? (*Sighs.*) Never mind that. Never mind what Stephen . . . (*He sighs. He lights the joint and inhales. He is overwhelmed. To phone.*) Look, Amy, I know that you're rattled, but there's nothing I can do right at this minute, see? We don't really have proof. (*Sighs.*) I'm well aware how he seemed. I know that all roads, they seem to lead to, but . . . (*Irritated.*) Because there's too much at stake here, *for me*, don't you get it? (*Coughs explosively.*) He *is*? He has *what*?

He sighs. He closes his eyes, taking the phone from his ear. He smokes. He opens his eyes. He has the unhinged look of a sleepless obsessive.

(*Exhausted, to phone.*) Fine. I said, fine. I said I'll wait right here, Amy, but it better be good. (*Sighs.*) I know you're not to blame. Let me call you back later.

He hangs up. He puts his head on the table. He stays like that a moment.

(*Sitting upright.*) What is it with these kids? What is it with their attitude . . . this pandemic . . . malaise? The Great God Bacchus descends on them. But that's only half the story . . .

A bell rings.

(*Surprised.*) Stephen? (*Apprehensive.*) Scott?

He stubs out the joint and pockets it. He fans the air with his hands.

Nicola *comes on. She is wearing a long overcoat and carrying a big, expensive designer-handbag. She eyes him a moment.*

Alan (*overly cheerful*)   Hey, you!

Nicola (*stopping short, suspicious*)   What happened?

Alan   What happened, what happened? There's a malaise is what happened. I . . . (*Struggling to stand.*) Lovely to see you. Aren't you looking fantastic?

He manages to stand. There's an ugly red wine stain smeared across his jacket. He's evidently very stoned.

Nicola   Swellegant.

Alan   What? (*Noticing the stain.*) Oh.

He steadies himself against the chair. **Nicola** *watches him, with disapproval.*

Alan   Come to think of it, actually, some water . . .

He goes off.

Nicola *takes a deep breath. She looks around the room, appalled. She puts her handbag down carefully. She sits down. Violent retching off.*

Nicola   Charming start to the morning. Another Sunday, I guess.

Alan *comes back on, with a glass of water. He drinks.*

Alan   Well, now, that's so much better. A dying man in the desert. (*Remembering.*) Oh, and *The Thirsty Ghost*, right . . . ?

Nicola   Excuse me?

Alan   Hold that thought . . .

He finishes the water. She looks at him coolly. He smiles benignly, forgetting whatever point he was thinking of making. She sighs. She picks up her handbag. She opens it. She takes out a small compact and begins touching up her make-up.

Alan (*putting the glass down*)   Now.

Nicola *looks at him, bewildered.*

Alan   Name for a bar, yes? (*Laughs.*) I mean, if I had my way . . .
(*Beat.*) Not that I'd run The Thirsty Ghost like this place. No,
I'd be trying to recreate a faded elegance; all walks of life. All
are welcome.

Nicola *looks at him with despair. She snaps the compact shut. She puts
it away.*

Nicola   *What*, will you tell me . . . I mean, have you gone *mad*?

Alan   Mad? What's mad about it?

Nicola *sighs. She stands up.*

Alan (*laughs nervously*)   Calm down, calm down. I can take a
hint. (*Flippantly.*) Now, don't you try to tell me it's the crashing-
out-on-the-couch business. I clearly remember that I ran that
one by you. It's about Richard's keys? Now, *we're all aware* that
the . . . champ is still driving, so you can't possibly blame me
for the fact that he cancelled that meeting with you and that
management guy, yeah? (*Hollow, numb.*) I don't know really
why you're so angry with me, Nicola. You think we're drifting
apart? (*Sadly.*) That's a possibility.

Nicola *looks at him a moment. She is a little thrown by this suggestion.*

Alan *sighs. He looks at his watch. He notices the megaphone.*

Alan   Look, on second thoughts . . . don't you have somewhere
to be?

Nicola   We had a date!

Alan (*lost*)   A date? What date?

Nicola   Then it wasn't a date. If *you* didn't think it was a
date, then it obviously wasn't. I thought we agreed that we'd
meet for breakfast.

Alan (*remembers*)   Oh.

Nicola   Now I find you ensconced and it appears that
you're . . . blotto. (*A little upset now.*) I've been sitting in Crumb

for the past twenty-five minutes. I tried calling you three times. Do you know what Crumb's like on a Sunday at this hour? (*Shocked.*) It's stuffed to the rafters with . . . with poseurs!

Alan   How'd your meeting with that management guy go? You said he'd got in touch with you.

Nicola (*exasperated*)   Oh, now, come on, just don't do that, all right?

Alan   Do what?

Nicola   You're feigning an interest!

Alan (*laughs*)   No, I'm not. (*Sighs.*) Yes, I am.

Nicola *looks at him, appalled.*

Alan (*sincere*)   I am exhausted here, okay? I'm dog tired and I . . . (*Sighs.*) You're out of the loop. You're out of the loop, so don't give me that look. I've had a lot on my plate here. (*Confused.*) And I can't help but feel that I somehow . . . deserve it . . .

Nicola *looks at him. She tries to appear agreeable.*

Nicola   Then, cool. You're forgiven. Boys will be boys, right?

She takes out her mobile phone and snaps it open.

I'm going to call us a taxi. You'll meet me halfway? We can go home and chill. I'll make us scrambled eggs, I think there's those olives left. We'll talk it through, like adults.

Alan *doesn't seem to agree.*

Nicola   Are you saying you're too wrecked to climb into a cab, Simms?

Alan *just sighs. He has no response.* **Nicola**'s *angry now. She snaps her phone shut. She sees the megaphone. She picks it up. It squeals with feedback.*

Nicola (*through the megaphone*)   ANYBODY ALIVE IN THERE, BUSTER? GIVE ME A SIGN IF YOU'RE LUCID!

Alan (*angry, trying to grab the megaphone*)   Stop that, okay! Will you stop? Would you quit?

Nicola *sighs. She puts the megaphone down. She turns away.*

Alan   It's not as if I'm relishing the prospect of staying here, Nicola. I'm not trying to avoid meeting you halfway. Somebody's coming over and I told them, I . . . (*Sighs, frustrated.*) Stephen's swinging by, he says he has developments . . .

Nicola   Bye.

Alan (*a little frantic*)   Look, *you're out of the loop*, love. What do you have to *do* that for, huh?

Nicola   Do what?

Alan (*irritated*)   Take everything in my life that doesn't involve *you* as some kind of affront; a personal slight?

Nicola (*hesitates*)   I don't do that.

Alan   Oh, you think? (*Laughs.*) It's as if me talking gets in your way. I mean, let's face it, your talking, it gets in mine. You talk about your things. I feign an interest. And then I talk about my things. And you feign an interest. And then, we talk, at cross purposes about two different things entirely, and then we get drunk and fall down and have pretty bad sex. And then you talk about something like bleaching your teeth and I drift off to sleep and I dream about . . . (*Beat.*) What do I dream about? (*Laughs.*) Well, I dream about this place. I dream I'm right here, with the people that come in. You're here. And Richard. Jonathan's here and the whole . . . select bunch. It appears I'm *denied* to dream of anything else. I dream about work.

Nicola *steps back to the couch, holding her bag with both hands. She is quiet, cautious, apprehensive . . . there is something about* **Alan** *she has never seen before.*

Nicola (*quietly*)   Fair enough. I'll sit down, then.

She sits down.

Alan   Ask me, you know, anything you want.

Nicola (*quietly*)   I think it's a bit unfair, some of what you said. I think that that thing, that thing you said about . . . *talking –*

Alan (*in wondrous amusement*)   Anything you damn like, Nicola. Have I sailed a canoe? Did I ever fly a kite?

Nicola (*ignoring him*)   I can recall very many conversations. I can recall . . . well, there were several. (*Tries to laugh.*) There was that time at the restaurant when the maître d', he . . . (*Frowns, laughs.*) Well, maybe, maybe, no. Let's not talk about that. But there were very many conversations that went long into the small hours. (*Haughty.*) As for bad sex, well . . .

Alan   You want to know what we talk about? We talk about Richard. *That's* the subject at hand, when you and I, when we're talking. And when we're *not* talking, well, what's the reason we're not? (*Laughs.*) We talk about Richard. We may laugh, we may bitch, it's his car, his new bistro, but at the end of the day it's about Richard now, isn't it? The wonder within that is Richard Carlisle. How he, and those other . . . those other brave pioneers: the magazine supplements, the merry song we all sing . . . (*Beat.*) And don't take me wrong, it's as much my fault as yours.

*He looks at **Nicola**. She has no retort really.*

Nicola   Did you ever . . . fly a kite?

Alan   Well, Nicola, you know: I have to say that I didn't.

*He rummages in his jacket pockets. He first produces **Amy**'s sunglasses. He scowls, replaces them. He rummages again. He finds the joint, he puts it in his mouth. But he can't find his lighter.*

Nicola (*still a little dazed*)   You need a light?

Alan   Hit me.

Nicola (*rummaging in her handbag*)   I'm not sure if I'm supposed to be appalled or impressed, Alan. I certainly don't recall you smoking joints before.

She produces a lighter and gives him a light.

Alan   Thank you.

Nicola   Pleasure.

Alan *closes his eyes, inhales deeply from the joint. He sways a little on his feet.*

Nicola (*slowly*)   Are you saying that we . . . ? (*Beat.*) Look, just
what is it you're saying here? (*Struggling.*) So, you're suggesting
that we . . . we are *lacking* somehow. It's about me and Richard?
Because that thing with the keys, well, I was bound to get
upset . . .

Alan *smokes, oblivious.*

Nicola (*appalled*)   What *happened* here last night? What's going
on in your head? What is it you think you somehow . . . deserve?

Alan (*laughs*)   I can't cut it.

Nicola   Cut it? Cut what?

Alan   I'm saying I can't cut it, Nicola. I'm saying enough,
I am finished. I am saying to you, I've reached the end of the
line. Now, you might simply think this is my hangover talking,
but . . . (*Considers this option.*) No. No, it's not that. (*Beat.*) Amy,
you know: she had some harsh words with me yesterday.
(*Laughs.*) Dull? I think not. You would look at him, wouldn't
you – he's pretty much like the next guy. (*Laughs.*) I've been
thinking . . . all this . . . it might lead to *something*. If I keep my
head above water, I'll be vibrant, dynamic, well, then the day
will come, when I measure up, too, right? (*Laughs.*) I recognise
now it's a phantasm, isn't it?. I recognise now *I've been sent down
the creek* . . . (*Beat.*) So I don't really know what you want me to
be, Nicola, but I can tell you for sure that I won't be becoming
that guy any time soon.

Nicola   You think I want you to be Richard?

Alan   Everybody wants to be Richard. (*Shrugs.*) Well, all right,
not everybody. (*Defensively.*) Most of the people who come in here.
Most of those kids, whole swathes of the south side . . . (*Beat.*)
He owns Lotus and Amber. He owns Crumb and Bamboo.
I've been playing this part here. My heart's been wrapped in ice.

Nicola *nods, shyly. This seems to register with her.*

Alan   And you're *doomed* in this city, if you're not cut out for
it, aren't you?

Nicola   People, they think that there's something wrong with
you.

Alan   People, they think that you're a waste of space.

Nicola *looks at him a moment. She walks straight up to him. She reaches for the joint.*

Nicola   Give me that.

She takes the joint. She smokes.

So, you're secretly gay and you're banging Stephen, then, is it?

Alan *(appalled)*   Excuse me?

Nicola   Or maybe it's *Richard* – Richard's banging you. *(Laughs.)* It's a joke.

Alan   Hah!

Nicola *(very stoned now, skittish)*   Would you chill?

Alan *shrugs. He tries to chill.*

Nicola *(still smoking)*   Okay. Okay. Here's my diagnosis. Now, I don't know exactly what went on here last night, but you're having your moment, and that's cool, that's cool. So, you're telling me now that you're not cut out for it. I'm presuming this concept also extends to me. *(Beat.)* Well, my diagnosis is we do one of two things. We either, A, accept the fact that we're both complete narcissists and, it would seem, both obsessed with Richard – which, I may stress, I am certainly not; if *that* be the case, well, we should definitely break up. Break up, keep it clean, my friends, your friends, the CDs, the whole business. *(Beat.)* Option B, though, however . . . are you listening to me?

Alan *(blasé)*   Look, the whole situation's about Jonathan's car . . .

Nicola   You need to step up, Simms! So, we've read the small print, it's your quarter-life crisis. So, this workaday world, it all seems like a sham to you. *(Laughs.)* We are chasing the rainbow. Very sharp. How astute. *(Beat.)* The rainbow's pretty at least. Life would be dead dull without it.

Alan *looks at her a moment.* **Nicola** *appears to have got through to him. She sighs, takes one last puff on the joint, drops it and stubs it out underfoot. She approaches him.*

Nicola   Okay, grand. Here's the deal. A moratorium on Richard. Let's have a complete blanket ban on discussing the man, yes? You're obsessed with the fact that you're meant to measure up. And now you are telling me that we . . . that we don't measure up either. Maybe, you know, we moved in too quickly. So, the relationship, it's not . . . it isn't scaling the heights. We've only known each other a few months, Alan. And as regards *talking*, we don't have time to talk, do we?

Alan (*in agreement, it's tempting*)   A moratorium on Richard?

Nicola   I am offering you a once-in-a-lifetime giveaway deal, Simms. What can I say? I marched straight in here, I was totally insensitive, I was still pretty furious about Friday night. You're in your own space, it looks like you've been through the mill here. So, we both rag about Richard. (*Laughs, embracing him.*) So, we've been living, you know . . . well, we're vicarious, aren't we? A moratorium on Richard. And let's just get on with living.

Alan *looks at her a moment. They kiss.* **Alan** *scowls, he turns away.*

Alan   Richard did it.

Nicola   What?

Alan   Richard, he did it. He beat up the kid! (*Awkwardly.*) Okay, I'm not saying he personally did the kicking himself, but . . .

Nicola   What? Are you kidding me?

Alan   Well, I tried to tell you that you were out of the loop, Nicola.

Nicola *looks at him in shock a moment. She opens up her handbag.*

Nicola   You want a muffin?

Alan (*ignoring her*)   It's about Jonathan's car. (*Irritated.*) Now, I'm going to speed through this, right, because it's been driving me crazy.

Nicola *unwraps the muffin.*

Alan   The keys that I found here belong to Jonathan. One of the Polish girls recognised them. Now, I got Jonathan's car registration from a parking ticket that I found from inside and I gave it to Stephen, because he had a hunch, and he made a call, see? And it turns out, you see, that the car's been impounded. Now, because Jonathan's away, at the fat-camp, okay, logically we can assume that no one can remove the said car from the pound without the keys, do you get it? (*Laughs.*) I mean, they're not going to let some random stranger just break into a car that's secure in a pound, are they? And I have the things still! That's bullet point number one.

Nicola   Jonathan's coming home on June 21st.

Alan *looks at her a moment. He's impressed.*

Nicola   So . . . ?

Alan   The keys have been lying here since last Sunday night. Scott, he came in here, he was waving a knife around. As far as I could ascertain, he was looking for something. So, let's go back to last Sunday. The night of the flood. Let's say Scott was here, yes? Let's say there was Scott and his friend Jeff Boston.

Nicola *tries to interject.*

Alan   Just . . . Just, please. I think I remember Scott being here but the place was packed, wasn't it, I can't be certain. Now, let's say Scott, or his friends, they had the keys, yes. I'm saying Jonathan's car, it's parked outside, Nicola. Let's say Scott, or this . . . Boston they're dropping something off. It's in the car. Now, it had been bucketing down for three days and three nights, hadn't it? All of a sudden, there's water spilling in every place. We had to clear everyone out fast; it was a hazard, the wiring. Now, let's say in the rush, the keys get misplaced . . .

Nicola   Misplaced?

Alan   I'm saying the kid loses them, Nicola. They get dropped on the floor, something stupid like that. Somebody else kicks them across the room. I'm saying that the keys, they get lost in the flood, yeah? Now, while the water's spilling in here, the car, it gets clamped, it gets towed away. We know, for a fact, that it's in a lot, right? Our enterprising young friend has maxed-out his luck now. What can he do? It isn't his car. Now, because *he* was supposed to deliver, you see, whatever's in the car, or pass it on to someone here – a third party – the *third party* beats the crap out of Scott, right? Amy was just the excuse, she blacked out, she's depressive. (*Heavily.*) Scott couldn't get back the keys. The place was under three foot of water. Friday morning, you see, I was the first one in here . . .

Nicola *looks at him a moment.*

Nicola   You're saying Richard's the third party?

Alan   I can't be sure at this point. But it seems to make sense, doesn't it?

Silence.

Nicola   Well, I suppose if it's true I don't see the big problem with that.

Alan (*laughs*)   You . . . ? What?

Nicola   Well, you see, you're confusing two things here. You are confusing a malicious *child*, blaming your sister, with . . . (*Beat.*) Well, with Richard beating the bollocks out of a not-very-nice boy. Now, let's say that Richard had, like, I don't know . . . like five Patrick Frame, five *designer suits* in there . . .

Alan   It's got nothing to with Patrick Frame suits!

Nicola   Calm down.

Alan   Whatever's in the damn car must be something illegal. It must be, you see, because otherwise, Scott . . . (*Beat, nervously.*) Scott needs to get the car back by June 21st. Because otherwise, see, Uncle Jonathan would be party to whatever's in the said car, and Jonathan . . . well, he's a civilised man.

Nicola *looks at him a moment. She folds her arms.*

Nicola   So, this changes things, does it?

Alan   Yes, I would say that this changes things. This is the world that I walk in. Richard has clout and I'm . . . I'm just . . . (*Weakly.*) You want to tell me now, maybe, what I'm supposed to do – shop him?

Nicola (*looks at him a moment*)   You want the muffin? I can't eat it.

Alan *looks at her. He tries to smile. Silence.*

Nicola   I slept with him one other time, Alan. It was the night of that flood. A week ago, yes. You'd been like a ghost, I . . . (*Irritated.*) You kept constantly inferring I was sleeping with Richard. You were obsessed with those kids, I . . . (*Beat.*) He caught me unawares. I guess I needed the boost. Well, to be honest with you, really, it wasn't as if we *slept* . . .

Alan   I had sex on the couch with one of the Polish girls.

Nicola (*arms folded, amused*)   Oh! Oh, well, oh really . . . !

Alan (*defensively*)   I mean, at least, in the moment, I almost felt . . . something. (*Grimly.*) This isn't good, Nicola. What kind of world do we walk in?

Nicola (*shrugs*)   Well, since you asked: I do sort of have a plan.

Alan (*grimly*)   Richard returned my call yesterday. I'm figuring, at this point, Scott has spoken to Richard, and he has told Richard I'm making trouble. Richard calls me back, he's *lovely* to me. I calmly tell Richard I think the kid's up to something. I tell him about the knife, how I think the kid's dangerous. I tell Richard *I think* that Scott had 'borrowed' Jonathan's car. I ask Richard if, maybe, he might know something about that. There's a pause. He says, 'No.' 'Well, all right, then,' I say. 'It was just a hunch.' Two minutes later, the phone goes again. It's Richard. And he's changed his tune this time, hasn't he, it now 'appears on reflection' he recalls something, after all. He says that he'd seen Jonathan's car *parked on the street* Thursday or Friday. But that's impossible, isn't it? Because the car's in the lot.

Nicola   Then, he's lying . . . ?

Alan   Well, he knows s*omething* for certain. Let's say I go to the police. Or I get that car open. Let's say there's something in it. (*Beat.*) Well, I'm asking you again, what am I supposed to do, Nicola? Because this relates to you and I, moratorium on Richard or no moratorium. I go to the police, I tell them

I'm . . . rattled. I let them sort it out, and should it get back to Richard. . . . (*He sighs.*) Well, if Richard's involved, I'm sure he'll muscle his way out of it. And regardless of whether he is or he isn't, I'll still have to tell them that Richard was letting those kids drink here. Richard and I will have reached the end of the line. He'll cut the ties with you, too, most likely. (*Hesitant.*) Unless, of course, you leave me.

Nicola   You mean this is some kind of test?

Alan   I didn't plan it this way. But it seems – me or him.

Silence. A bell rings.

Nicola (*alarmed*)   Who's that now?

Alan   That will be Stephen. (*Grimly.*) Now I'm not condoning for a minute what he did here last night, okay? Stephen's decided to make some trouble for himself. The man took his stand, I played no hand or part in it. But Amy rang me a few minutes ago . . . he's asked to come see me. (*Scowls.*) According to Amy, he has something . . . more. And if Stephen has news, well, then we can nail Richard, can't we? I mean, there's no sense doing anything unless we can prove it. (*Sighs.*) Stephen! Hey, Stephen! Stephen, we're in here.

Stephen *comes on. He seems exhausted. He is wearing the same suit. It is crumpled. The similarity between* **Alan** *and* **Stephen** *should appear evident.*

Alan   Good morning.

Stephen   Bruised. But unbowed.

Alan *tries to smile. He looks to* **Nicola** *nervously.*

Stephen (*amused, to* **Alan**)   And evidently still sober, unlike some people here. After the drama last night, then, did you hit the bottle? (*Turning to* **Nicola**.) Lucky for me that he crashed out here, isn't it? I don't have a number at your place of residence . . .

He smiles. He looks at **Nicola**. *She finds the situation unbearable. She looks at* **Alan** *a moment.* **Nicola** *goes off.*

Alan (*calling after her*)   We'll talk later, yes?

Stephen   That girl should eat.

Alan (*shocked*)   Sorry?

Stephen   She should eat. She should eat. She's wasting away.

Alan   Nicola eats.

Stephen   Man cannot live on cappuccino alone, Alan.

He shrugs. **Alan** *notices the muffin. He scowls.*

Alan   You all right, then, are you? They didn't rough you up?

Stephen   I slept like an infant.

Alan (*exasperated*)   And . . . ?

Stephen (*eyeing him a moment, amused*)   Have you been plugging away at the old . . . (*Mimes smoking a spliff.*) . . . joystick, then, huh?

Alan   Joystick?

Stephen   Giggle-spliff.

Alan (*seemingly stoned again*)   Look, I've never, in my whole life, heard them called 'joysticks' before. I accept, you might think you know one or two things about *drink* . . . (*Irritated.*) Look, what's the evidence? What's the evidence, Stephen? Because if there's something you can *prove*, well, then, that's Amy, she's free and clear. (*Defensively.*) Otherwise, buddy, this door would be shut to you . . .

He looks at **Stephen**. **Alan** *can't stand his ground. He finds his glass of wine.*

Alan   You've got something to tell me? About Scott? About Richard?

Stephen   How do you think Amy feels that I spent the night in the cells last night?

Alan   How does she feel? How do you imagine she feels?

Stephen (*sadly*)   She'll take it hard.

Alan   Don't you get some idea, now, that we're on the same side, right? Don't you start to think just because you're sober . . . (*Laughs, awkwardly.*) Now, whatever my opinion on Richard, he . . . (*Sighs.*) I mean, if all of this, if it's some big scheme of yours . . .

Stephen (*amused*)   A big scheme? A big scheme? What on this earth could I have to possibly gain?

Alan (*irritated*)   Then what happened *last night*? What was the point of it, well?

Stephen *finds his megaphone. He picks it up. He seems pleased.*

Stephen   Merely a show of solidarity. It was a civic . . . revolt.

Alan (*frustrated*)   What was it supposed to accomplish?

Stephen   I want to reiterate. Amy played no hand or part.

Alan   I know. She tried to warn me.

Stephen   I am simply saying that if something should happen to me. I'm a creature of habit. Of emotion. Of impulse. I don't always think these things sensibly through. The uprising felt . . . natural. Usurping the throne, huh? (*Shrugs.*) Well, then, have it your way. I know we're against the clock here.

He moves closer to **Alan***. He puts a hand on his arm.*

Stephen   It's all tied in with the school.

Alan   The school?

Stephen (*gravely*)   Yes.

Alan   How?

Stephen (*noticing the papers*)   Seems to me that us greys, we think alike, hmmm? You've been up half the night leafing back through old papers. Stumble upon anything?

Alan   There've been a couple of incidents involving kids at that Institution, yes.

Stephen   Incidents?

Alan   Tabloid stuff, you know. Kids getting into fights. Drinking too much. (*Beat.*) There's a malaise as you said. Kids get pissed up, they're tanked, they get cranky . . .

Stephen (*enjoying this greatly*)   Richard's on the board.

Pause.

Alan   What?

Stephen   The board. Of the school. You can check it out for yourself.

Alan (*a little threatened*)   It . . . ?

Stephen   The Advanced Institution has a 'mentoring' scheme. For promising students, they hand-pick the elite. Richard's what they call a 'Big Brother in Business'.

Alan (*rather shocked*)   Where did you hear this?

Stephen   A woman at the bus station. She showed me how to use Google.

Alan *stares at* **Stephen** *a moment in disbelief.*

Alan (*embarrassed*)   Well, our broadband is down. It must have been the flood.

Stephen   What do you want me to do, give you his head on a plate?

Alan *hesitates. He doesn't like* **Stephen**'s *tone.* **Stephen** *looks at him, frustrated. He puts the megaphone to his mouth.*

Stephen (*through the megaphone*)   RICHARD CARLISLE IS A LIAR AND A THIEF! RICHARD CARLISLE IS QUITE LIKELY A PEDERAST. REGARDLESS OF THIS, THE MAN, HE HAS MULES WHO DO HIS BIDDING! THE EVIDENCE, SIR, IS IN YOUR POSSESSION. GO DOWN TO THAT POUND. FIND AND OPEN THAT VEHICLE.

Nicola *comes on, disturbed by the noise.*

Stephen (*through the megaphone*)   SO, WHAT, NOW, SO WHAT? YOU'RE A VACILLATOR? IT'S A QUARTER-LIFE CRISIS, IS THAT WHAT YOU'D CALL IT? YOU'VE KNOWN FOR A LONG TIME THERE'S SOMETHING ILL. YOU KNOW IT. YOU *FEEL*? YOU'RE

AFRAID OF LOSING YOUR JOB? OR THAT YOUR WOMAN WILL
LEAVE YOU? A MAN IS A MAN BECAUSE HE HAS A CODE, MAN. A
MAN IS A MAN WHEN HE STANDS UP FOR WHAT'S RIGHT . . . !

Alan (*angry*)   And what are you, huh? A drunkard!

Stephen (*through the megaphone*)   THE GREAT GOD DIONYSUS?
WHY SHOULD HE TAKE THE FALL?

Alan   Stop it!

He struggles with **Stephen** *to wrench the megaphone away.*

Stephen (*struggling to maintain control of the megaphone*)   THIS
SPLENETIC CITY . . .

Alan *pulls the megaphone away.* **Stephen** *takes back control.*

Stephen   . . . BLINDNESS!

Alan *wrenches the megaphone from* **Stephen**. *He throws it to the floor.
He turns and finds* **Nicola** *watching them.*

Alan *and* **Stephen** *breathe heavily.* **Stephen** *picks up his megaphone.*

Stephen (*sighs, embarrassed*)   Very good. Very good.

Alan   You've given me nothing here. Other than a pain in
my skull.

Stephen   Is that right? (*Shrugs.*) Well, I'm going. I'm gone.
Home, James, to . . . Amy.

Stephen *and* **Alan** *look at one another.*

Stephen   You be nice to your sister. You treat her with
courtesy, treat her with respect. She's a fragile one, isn't she?
The girl can be snappish . . . but that is of the malaise. (*Beat.*)
My time is short now, I feel. Should I somehow succeed in
avoiding the gaolhouse, well, this sobriety business, I don't
think that it'll take, you know. Bells, they keep ringing, the
ginger ale makes me gassy. I'm going to have to let go of her.
For her own sake, of course. Or rather, I will let, *I will let her let
go of me.* (*Sadly.*) I can say that we loved. We can say that, at
least. I want it on the record, dipsomania or otherwise . . .
(*Beat.*) I may have been a rogue. A malingerer, surely . . .

(*Shrugs.*) Opt-in or opt-out. One always has the option. It's the
wilderness, otherwise. (*Beat.*) Look, just check in on her a bit
over the next weeks, please? I can't imagine she's going to take
the separation too well. (*He hesitates.*) By the way, just to warn
you, I'd say that boy will be back. Richard knows you're
involved now. I could see it on his face. But he'll sit this one out,
he mustn't be tainted. The kid's all on his own. And should the
worst happen come June 21st, it will be Scott that I fear shall
get thrown the wolves. This is surely a pickle. (*Cheerfully.*) But
the ball's in your court, man. So, it seems it's all about *you*, and
not Amy at all, eh?

He goes off.

Silence.

Alan   He came down.

Nicola (*numb*)   I choose you.

Alan   Stephen came down here with his *friends* last night,
Amy was already here, see? So, he assembles, I don't know,
maybe *twenty-five* people, they drift in one by one. Stephen tells
me later he'd done it all for my benefit, just in case Scott . . .
or Richard, they chose to launch an offensive. They're old lads,
you see, that Richard's turfed out from here. They're punk kids
with haircuts, who've seen Richard on TV, and have taken a
scorn to him. I mean, it's the League Against Richard, do you
see what I'm saying? Now, God only knows how they all got
past Security, but Richard, he's . . . he's none too pleased, you
can imagine. Amy comes up, she grabs my arm. 'I'm sorry,'
she says. 'There's nothing I can do.' She high-tails it out of
here. Then Stephen's on the table, barking out abuse, and
there's the accordion, a girl with a saxophone. It's like . . . a
huge tuneless din . . . and they're all singing this dirge, it's a
sea-shanty, something, and Stephen is there, leading them on.
He's sober apparently. It doesn't seem to make a difference!
(*Laughs.*) Now, I've got one eye on the door, I mean, my hands
were tied here. I'm expecting young Scott to burst in any
minute. Richard, he turns, he gives me a look. As if to say,
'Deal with it.' Then he gets on the phone.

Nicola   And what happened?

Alan   Well, I just stood there, didn't I? Richard called the police. They arrived. Hauled them out.

Silence.

Nicola   Those things Stephen said? You really think it's that *heavy*?

Alan   Look, I'm going to call the police. What choice do I have here?

Nicola   But . . .

Alan   What?

Nicola (*defensive*)   Well, I've said it once, haven't I? There you are: I choose you.

They look at one another. This confuses him.

Well, it's not like you've said 'I choose you' too!

Alan *takes the keys out. He puts them on the table. He stares at them.*

A bell rings.

Alan (*clutching at straws, frantic*)   Stephen, *you* take the keys! Tell the cops *you* found them!

He picks up the keys.

Nicola   Alan, wait.

Alan *goes off.*

Nicola   Brilliant, that's that, then. Back to the departure lounge, Nicola.

She opens her handbag. She takes out an envelope. She opens the envelope. She takes out a folded letter. She tears it efficiently in two. She returns the torn pieces to her handbag.

Alan *comes back. She just looks at him.*

Nicola (*extremely defensive*)   I choose you! I choose you!

Alan   I thought I heard something. It must have been the wind. (*He puts the keys back on the table. Slowly.*) Look, do *you* think that it's possible that we turn a new page here? You think there's something – because I think I need something. We could . . . I dunno. There could be some substance here, right? Some substance, you know, do you hear what I'm saying? (*Increasingly distressed.*) I mean, do you think that there's *something* . . . something real here between us?

Nicola   Alan.

She looks at him, scowls. She opens her handbag. She takes out the torn halves of the letter. She gives them to him.

Alan   What's this?

Nicola   The point that I'm making is that it's already torn.

Alan   What's this? A work thing? You tore it up?

Nicola   It's already torn, Alan. That's the issue here, okay?

Alan *looks at her a moment. He assembles the letter.*

Nicola   It's a two-bedroom duplex overlooking Royal Way. It's on the top floor, etc. It has gas central heating, oak-panelled floors. There's a sauna and gym, a view, so they tell me. Apparently, you look out straight over the canal. Now George *said* we could get in at the price at the top there. I mean, the whole complex, it's not even on the market yet, see? (*He looks at her a moment.*) There's no work thing, okay? Well, there might be, in a few months, George has dozens of projects. (*Cringes.*) Richard is friends with this guy – George Mason. He's the 'management consultant'. Richard was *supposed* to introduce us on Friday night. He called, as I said, and I don't know if it's still on, but apparently *George*, as a favour to Richard . . .

Alan (*appalled, his head in his hands again*)   Ah, Nicola.

Nicola   But the point is, you see, I tore it up! (*She takes the letter back and tears it in four.*) And now I'm tearing it again!

Silence.

By the time they're on the market, they'll be up ten per cent.

Alan   And if, you and I, we were to buy this place, we . . . ?

Nicola   A moratorium on Richard! I thought we'd already agreed!

Alan   Yes, but what I mean is, what would we be doing this *for*?

Nicola (*laughs, awkwardly*)   Well, what do you think we'd be doing it for, Alan? I think we both know we can't go it alone – financially speaking. Call it a partnership. If the relationship blossoms, well then, fair game. There'd be solicitors, then, mortgage advisers. Well, there'd certainly be plenty to talk about, wouldn't there? And should we part on our merry way, well, we just split the winnings. (*Beat, irritated.*) But as, anyway, as I said, I choose you, you see, don't I?

Alan   And then we're bound to him. Richard does us this favour, and then we're bound to him. We press ahead, there'll be the repayments. And then I turn a blind eye to whatever's supposed to be going on here . . .

They look at one another. **Nicola** *rises. She offers her hand.*

Nicola   Let's go home. Have crap sex.

She looks at him. He doesn't move. She sighs. She picks up her handbag. She goes off.

Silence.

Alan (*a shout*)   I mean, sooner or later, there'll be blood spilt, you know! Stephen says it's a malaise! There's going to have to be violence! (*He rises unsteadily. He tops up his glass. Regretting it.*) Nicola! (*Beat.*) Nicola!

He stands there defiantly, with the glass in hand. With his suit dishevelled, his shirt untucked, he could almost pass for a younger version of **Stephen**. *He is struck by a tremor. It terrifies him.*

Alan   Sparrows hitting the skylight! This whole place gets flooded!

Scott *comes on, in the shadows. He's off his head totally: some kind of hallucinogenic psychosis, presumably drug-related. His clothing is torn. There are cuts on his face.* **Alan** *places his hand over the keys before*

Scott *can see them.* **Scott** *is breathing heavily, his face is a contortion of envy and rage.*

Nicola *comes on. She does not notice* **Scott**. *She is very upset.*

Nicola   Alan.

She takes his arm. He seems oblivious.

Look, you need to get in a cab here. You seriously don't look well.

Scott   It's not my fault. It's Jeffrey's.

Nicola *turns, in fright.*

Scott   Let them take Jeffrey, why can't they do that? Why can't they find Jeffrey? (*Laughs.*) Have you seen him? It's his bag. Let them have . . . Boston! He's the one who's so rad. (*He notices* **Alan** *and* **Nicola**.) They threw me out of Lotus. I've been walking the streets. I think I saw the sun spinning. (*Regarding* **Nicola**.) Is that her? She's not bad. My name is Scott, I think you need a younger lover. Check! I see you, baby. How about a lap-dance? Don't you worry, I'm flush. (*He puts his hand in his pocket, takes out a handful of change and looks at the coins.*) Oh. Bloody Mary. It appears we are spent, folks. Coming down. Coming down. (*Beat.*) You are vanishing now, right before my eyes. You are . . . merging, it seems, growing fins, are they wings?

Alan *reveals the keys. But* **Scott**'s *too far gone to notice. He backs away as* **Alan** *approaches him.*

Alan   Is this what you want? Well, then, come here, you prick!

Scott *goes off.* **Alan** *goes off, in pursuit.*

Nicola   Alan!

She slumps to the floor. She seems very upset.

It begins to rain.

Act Four

A flash flood: rain becomes torrential as the set revolves one final time. Distant dogs bark. An ambulance siren as the rain becomes more ferocious.

The rain stops suddenly. The set is back to 'first positions'. Lights up on the 'new' apartment. It's a fortnight later.

Alan *is showing* **Amy** *around the 'new' apartment.*

The 'new' apartment is much the same as the old one – the balcony and the bulk of the furniture are all exactly the same. On the coffee table there are two cups and saucers. The plinth by the balcony remains, but the plant is gone. Unusually, the ivy also remains, but is now hanging in a different position.

Amy   It's very nice. Very . . . spacious.

Alan   We had the mortgage fast-tracked. We were in in less than two weeks. And, of course the city's right there, isn't it? Literally, on our doorstep. Nicola, well . . . she's thrilled to bits. (*Beat.*) We both are.

Amy (*looking at him a moment*)   As we can all plainly see.

Alan (*pointing over the balcony*)   Do you see that old grey building down there? That's the place that I'm talking about. (*Beat.*) Of course it's all just hypothetical.

Amy (*sitting down*)   Lovely cups.

Alan *looks at her a moment. He feigns a smile.*

Amy   What? Did I say something?

Alan (*cheerfully*)   Speak your mind if you wish, Amy. We're all friends here. If you're going to give me the tirade about having a code again . . . (*Laughs.*) Well, this is all above board. An opportunity turned up. We took it while we could. (*Shrugs, laughs.*) Of course, you should be aware, it's far from happy endings, I mean, the repayments alone, they're . . . As for my plans to try and take out that lease . . . it's a dream. Hypothetical. Excellent location, though; it won't be empty long. You want a biscuit or something? Nicola's brought some of those luxury crisps.

Amy   I've cut out all sugar. All confectionery, everything.

Alan (*looks at her. He is beaming with optimism*)   Of course, if you want to discuss what went on, we can do that now, Amy. We're adults here, aren't we?

Amy   Well, it's a tragedy, isn't it? I resent the whole thing actually.

Alan   Resentment's no use, Amy.

Amy   I resent how I'm being made a pariah like this. (*Scowls.*) That might sound self-centred, I know, but I can't help but feel that . . . (*Sighs.*) Not that I'm surprised that the media's all over it. (*Sighs.*) There was a picture of me in at least three of the papers. I look loutish, harangued . . . (*Sighs.*) And I feel wretched to say this, because I know how it'll sound, but the whole sordid interest is because he's middle class. He was the *Übermensch*, wasn't he? The blond, blue-eyed boy. (*Scowls.*) If it had been some runt in a hoodie with no arse in his trousers, his death would be . . . commonplace . . .

Alan (*trying to be helpful*)   Your medication, then, Amy . . . when's it supposed to kick in?

Amy   I never went back on them. I mean, I know what I said . . . I promised you, fine . . . (*Sighs.*) I got through this much, didn't I? (*Doubtful.*) Do you think – well, you know – I mean, if I really hit him . . . ?

Alan   You never touched the kid, Amy!

Amy   Yes, well, I don't think I did. But I can't be certain. It turned out there was nothing on that CCTV tape. The school had decided to keep the whole thing an internal matter. We can't blame ourselves, can we? Do we think we know what goes on inside other people's heads? Do we think we know why people do what they do?

They look at one another.

Alan   You want a hug?

Amy (*laughs nervously*)   Well, if that's book by you.

They embrace.

Alan (*looking to the window*)   Of course it would just be a question of securing the lease. I could probably get help drawing up the business plan . . .

Amy   You are!

Alan   What?

Amy   You're on Prozac!

Alan   Amy.

Amy   You are! I can tell! I suppose that partly explains it, that zoned-out expression, this weird kind of . . . optimism –

Alan (*a little rattled now*)   Look, I'll go through it at the inquest, nobody's accusing me here. *Neither* of us, Amy, is to blame for what went on. Scott came back to the bar, he looked like he was going to attack me and Nicola. He was off his head, totally, he bolted outside . . . I followed him out there to get some answers, you see . . . He ran for it, I . . . (*Sighs.*) Look, it's been a hell of a month, Amy. On top of that, we moved house.

Silence.

Amy (*shrugs*)   Well, we float on.

Alan   The tablets I'm taking are just a temporary measure. It's not Prozac, okay? They're just new on the market. And, well, since you must know, they haven't even kicked in yet, so I don't know for the life of me how you could possibly tell. (*Rising.*) I just need to get some air for a minute. There's some nice crisps inside. Look around. Help yourself.

He gets up and goes to the balcony. He has a slight limp. He looks up at the ivy.

This is a new build, you know. Walls are solid concrete. There's no wood up there, no dry rot or anything. The building's been surveyed . . .

Amy   And you noticed the . . . feature, but you moved in anyway?

Alan   We bought it straight off the plans. (*Shrugs.*) It's not a complete disaster. Just more cash to shell out.

Amy   Alan, the kid's dead.

Alan *turns and looks at her, a little shaken by her bluntness.*

Amy (*defensively*)   I'm only stating the obvious. But it's . . . sobering, isn't it?

Alan   I know the kid's dead! Everyone knows the kid's dead!

Silence.

Amy (*awkwardly*)   Anyway, that's not particularly what I came here to talk about . . .

Alan   I'm doing my best to move on here now, aren't I? As the inquest will hear, there were no wounds on his body. No bruises, of course, other than those that were already there. He leapt off that bridge, in the full view of over forty people, and I was at the other side of town at that exact moment, wasn't I? (*Beat.*) Yes, I followed him out. I followed him out, but as I've already told everyone . . .

Amy   Something came over you and you passed out on the street.

Alan   So?

Amy (a *little awkwardly*)   Well, it seems to run in the family, this passing-out thing, doesn't it?

Alan *looks at her. He's lost for words.*

Amy   It's just, this past fortnight or so, I've been giving it thought. The passing-out, I mean, the fact that we both . . . (*Beat.*) Oh, I've had panic attacks, they're a dime a dozen really. But this blacking-out business, I . . . (*Beat.*) Well, you've got to take it as a sign. You've got to take it as a sign that the course you've been steering, it's . . . (*Laughs.*) A few hours before I had my . . . episode, Stephen and I . . . Stephen and I, we met for lunch on a bench by the canal where he sometimes likes to visit. I was feeling very depressed about going in to teach. We watched the traffic snail by, bumper to bumper. Stephen squeezed my hand and he said to me, 'You can opt in or opt out, Amy.' Which was terribly sweet, but it's nonsense, of course. Stephen's a romantic, he has no sense of the real world . . .

Alan   You want my opinion, you're better off without him.

Amy   I suppose these days that's what it comes down to. (*Sighs.*) How can we opt out? How can you opt out and still choose to live here? You'll end up like a mad person, standing on the street, blurting out slogans about how the world isn't fair. And the powers-that-be will say, 'What's the matter with you? Don't you have opportunities?' (*Sighs, frustrated.*) Oh, don't ask me. But there were about a thousand things wrong with me teaching those . . . horrors, and I guess at that moment at least something made sense. (*Laughs.*) I'm the one who is ill? I am the one?

Noises off.

Alan   Look, Nicola doesn't know about the pills, all right? I haven't broached the subject yet . . . and I prefer if you –

Amy   Well, I should be hitting the road anyhow.

Alan   It's just not a great idea to tell her right now, that's all. I mean, I only made the decision to go see the doctor . . . (*Sighs, laughs.*) She knows full well about everything else, of course . . .

Nicola *comes on. She is laden with shopping bags. She is wearing her most extravagant ensemble so far. Her hair is piled up high, sunglasses on her forehead.*

Nicola   Oh. (*Noticing* **Amy**.) Oh, hello, you!

Amy *acknowledges her.*

Nicola (*to* **Alan**)   Well, don't stand there, babes. Lend the shopper a hand . . .

Alan *approaches. He picks up some of the bags.*

Alan   Shopping.

Nicola (*to* **Amy**)   Oh, I know, sure, it's endless. (*Tousling* **Alan**'s *hair.*) What's with this, anyhow? You look so . . . windswept today.

She smiles broadly. They kiss.

How are you faring?

Amy   Fair to middling.

Nicola (*laughs, a release*)   You're telling me!

*She turns to **Alan**. She frowns, looking at his hair again. A thought strikes her. She turns back to **Amy**.*

Nicola   Oh! Good news!

Alan (*triumphant, oddly*)   You see!

Nicola   Now, steady on, buster! He's so giddy today. (*Approaching **Amy**.*) Well, I know that this might seem a tiny bit presumptuous. Best intentions, of course. I spoke to a colleague. His name is James Dukes. Well, he's in the process of delivering . . . I'm not too sure what it is, really. It's a partnership of some kind . . . People must come first . . . (*Snaps her fingers suddenly.*) A . . . social enterprise! Anyway, I made no bones about it, I said, 'Jimmy, Jimmy-boy. I have a dynamic candidate – '

Amy *looks to **Alan**, in panic.* **Nicola** *produces a business card.*

Nicola (*embarrassed*)   Look. It's got something to do with the whole counter-culture. James is expecting your call. There might be some kind of . . . job there.

Amy *looks at her, a little bashfully. She takes the card.*

Amy   That's very kind of you, thanks.

Nicola   Now, I know that the job is eighty-five miles away. But you could commute, I suppose, commute, or you could maybe . . . (*Laughs.*) People can sometimes mistake my intentions. But we all have to, well, you know what I mean . . .

Silence.

Did Alan tell you about his idea for The Thirsty Ghost?

Amy   I want to thank you again. For letting me use your old flat.

Nicola   Think nothing of it, girl. The rent's paid up till September.

Amy   Yes, but at least let me make . . . a contribution –

Nicola   The place is lying empty, someone should make use of it. (*Smiles.*) And, of course, fingers crossed, you'll have a job by then. (*Taking* **Alan***'s arm.*) Get you back with the programme. Maybe make some new friends.

Silence.

(*With bags again.*) Anyway, look, I've bought some new kitchen items for our new Shaker kitchen. That blue bag at your feet, have a look what's in that one.

Alan *produces an ornamental blue bowl from the bag.*

Nicola   The blue bowl, the blue bag. It's the subtle touches, now, isn't it? (*To* **Alan***.*) It belongs over there, I think. Yes, let me just . . . (*She puts the bowl on the plinth. She seems satisfied. Picking up her bags.*) Anyway, I'll leave you two to it. Could I get you a snack or something? Amy, you've eaten?

Amy   Well, no, to be honest, but I'm not really –

Nicola   Excellent plan! You know how I love to cook!

She goes off, with shopping bags.

Alan (*regarding anti-depressants*)   I know what you're thinking. She's completely drug free.

Nicola *comes on, a spatula in hand.*

Nicola (*brightly, to* **Alan**)   Oh, I ran into Jonathan. He's lost three and a half pounds!

She goes off.

Alan (*sighs, with difficulty*)   She's . . .

Amy   There's no need to explain, all right? I don't think she's trying to get rid of me.

Alan   Nicola's cool.

Amy   And, frankly, it doesn't matter if I'm won over or not, Alan. Given my track record, I'm hardly the one to talk.

Alan   Things are good here, things are better. (*Beat.*) I feel like I . . . (*Doubtful.*) I feel . . . (*Beat.*) Well, I can finally say this is me. Do you get it? This is the full package . . .

Silence.

You seen Stephen at all?

Amy (*quietly*)   Thankfully no. (*Shrugs.*) Although, the buzzer rang a few times over there at your old place. But I didn't pick up. (*Laughs.*) I reckoned, you know, it'd either be Stephen or a . . . journalist, maybe . . . (*Sighs.*) He called Mammy, though. A couple of times. She did as instructed. She wouldn't say where I was. I suppose, in my way, I've disappeared again, haven't I? But I worry a little, with him out there all alone. (*In wonder a little.*) It's really over.

Silence.

Nicola *comes on, with a handful of stones.*

Alan *looks at her quizzically.*

Nicola (*cheerfully*)   Stones.

Alan   Yes?

Nicola   For the bowl.

She empties the stones into the blue bowl. She goes off.

(*Off.*) Grub will just be a minute!

A bird flutters by.

Amy   Of course, the real thing that galls me was that I was so blind all the time. Stephen would get a notion, and I would just run with it. He'd get a notion in his head . . . (*Laughs.*) Don't you just hate that? 'Have pity on poor Amy, with no real will of her own.' I've seen enough alcoholics: they like to act out. They like to make stories up, they think it makes them important. And, of course, when he came home that Sunday, he was drunk as a skunk. Alcoholics, you know, they have their

'confabulations', and out of the clear blue sky . . . (*Laughs.*)
You fell for it too, didn't you? I mean, he led you right on, with
that conspiracy theory about that fella's car. (*Scowls.*) It was all
theatre, of course. Just a lot more convincing.

Alan   Scott wasn't himself. He was delusional certainly. He
must have been paranoid that his parents would find out that
he stole Jonathan's car. (*Shrugs.*) Scott never said a word about
Richard being involved, did he?

Silence.

Amy   I mean, you're telling me the truth? There was nothing
in the car, right?

Alan   We've been through this already . . . I brought Richard
down with me. We didn't hear till that night that Scott, he . . .
(*Sighs.*) I said to Richard, 'If you want to be trusted.' I went up
to the pound with him. He opened the car up, the boot and
everything . . .

Amy (*laughs, still a little shocked*)   They arrested him last year
for taking a slash in that shopping mall.

Alan   Stephen?

Amy   Apparently he had gout. He couldn't walk very far. He
got the probation act. Which almost certainly means now, in
the aftermath of that . . . riot –

Alan   Now, that was his own fault now, wasn't it?

Amy   It didn't help things, of course, that he had that kid's
knife on him. That was plain stupid. He'll go down this time,
certainly. He might even go to prison.

Nicola *comes on with a tray of food and a carafe of water. She is
wearing an apron. She gives them a big smile.*

Amy   I mean, just for the record, here's another example,
right? The mythical Jeff Boston. Stephen claimed he'd been
threatened. Then, he goes on to link Scott with this mysterious
other person, who we've never met, Alan, but all of us, all of
us, we swallow it, don't we? (*Still in disbelief.*) We indulged him

and why? (*Beat.*) I mean, I don't know, do I, maybe Jeffrey
exists . . . maybe he was the one who . . . (*Beat.*) Nobody, it
seems, can actually find him. The school claims they've no
record of him ever being enrolled there. Oh, there's a malaise,
I suppose . . . we all want explanations.

Nicola   It's an attempt at bruschetta, with a little salad on
the side. Help yourselves. (*Laughing.*) I have surrendered, you
see. Like the pinny?

She sits beside **Amy**. *She has no food for herself.*

Nicola   So, I take it we're still discussing the . . . blackness?

It begins to rain. **Alan** *eats.* **Nicola** *looks at him, concerned.*

Nicola   He's been taking it hard, you know. We both have, of
course. The poor child, his poor parents, they're beside themselves, totally. Jonathan, the poor man, he's been completely –

Alan   I feel much better!

Nicola   Calm down, babes. We know that.

Silence. **Amy** *begins to eat.*

Amy   Aren't you eating yourself, Nicola?

Nicola   Oh, no, no thank you. I've eaten already.

Amy *smiles politely.* **Alan** *gets up. He pours himself water. He walks
away.*

Nicola (*sotto voce, regarding* **Alan**)   The thirsty ghost here. He
seems okay to you, does he?

Amy   Yes. Yes, he does. Under the circumstances . . .

Nicola (*to* **Amy**, *sotto voce*)   Between you and me. I think that
he might be . . .

Amy   What?

Nicola   Depressed.

It rains harder. **Stephen** *comes on. He is soaked to the skin, but seems
in high spirits. He is wearing a colourful shirt – Hawaiian, most likely –
with some kind of hat, perhaps a boater. He is drunk.* **Alan** *sees him first.*

Stephen   The weather's bananas! People are driving like it's snowing!

They all look at him, bewildered.

Amy   Stephen, you . . . (*Exasperated.*) Why in God's name are you dressed like that, Stephen?

Stephen   Oh, you know me. Ever the optimist. The sun was blinding at noon. I predicted a scorcher. (*Shrugs.*) Shows how wrong you can be, of course.

He smiles at them all. He is clearly at his best. He takes his hat off and shakes the rain from it.

Alan   Stephen . . .

Stephen   No, no, no: honesty first, folks. Before indignation. (*To* **Nicola**.) I took the liberty of following you home, petal. It was a cheap shot, I admit, but I never said I wasn't cheap. (*To* **Amy**.) I had to find my love somehow. I've been like the wandering Jew. (*To* **Nicola**.) You didn't see me on the tram, then? My crossword in hand . . . the brim of my boater?

Nicola (*quietly*)   No.

Stephen (*regarding his clothing*)   Also an effective disguise, then. (*Triumphant.*) Still got it!

Amy (*half-amused, half-shocked*)   Stephen, come on, you can't be following the girl home.

Alan   You shouldn't be here at all, should you?

Stephen   He seems a bit snippy.

Amy (*exasperated, rising*)   Snippy? He's –

Alan (*urgent*)   Amy.

Amy (*sighs, approaching* **Stephen**)   You're going to get yourself a chill, Stephen, you can't be wearing those wet clothes. Alan, do you have a towel or something . . . ?

She stops in her tracks, she's falling back on old ways.

Stephen   No need for a towel. I'll dry out in the sun.

Amy *looks to* **Alan** *in despair.*

Stephen (*laughs, regarding the rain*)   Right in the eye of the storm, huh? Tremendous, tremendous.

He notices the ivy. He laughs uproariously.

Nice . . . pad, by the way.

Alan (*still stunned by* **Stephen**'*s entrance*)   How did you . . . ? Look, Stephen, you . . . I really don't think that Amy wants to speak to you –

Stephen   Oh, no? Taking action?

Alan   To be perfectly honest, none of us do. Amy, do you want me to ask him to leave?

Amy (*quietly*)   Let him speak.

Alan   Amy.

Amy   Let him speak, let him speak. For a minute, that's all. (*To* **Stephen**.) I owe you that, at least. (*Anxiously.*) But I'm not walking out with you, Stephen, so you better choose your words carefully.

Alan *sighs. He takes* **Nicola**'*s hand. They turn to go.*

Amy   Alan.

Alan *and* **Nicola** *both stop.*

Amy   Alan, if you don't mind I'd prefer if you . . .

Amy *and* **Alan** *look at one another.* **Nicola** *sighs and turns away.*

Amy (*to* **Stephen**)   I'd like him to stay, that's all. That's the deal, okay?

Nicola (*to herself*)   Bastards!

She goes off.

Silence. **Stephen** *seems in a world of his own.*

Amy (*exasperated*)   Well?

Stephen   Hmm?

Amy   What do you want to say to me, Stephen? You're running out of time here, you know.

Stephen *looks at her a moment. He remembers.*

Stephen   Aruba.

Amy   Uh. What?

Stephen   Aruba, Aruba. Aruba, Aruba, Aruba, Aruba! Me Google, you Google. Googleland, adieu! (*Shrugs.*) I considered Boston. I considered Berlin. Hang on a tick till you see what's in my pocket.

He rummages through his pockets. He finds his hip-flask, looks at it a moment, shrugs, puts it back in his pocket. He looks in another pocket. He produces an envelope and gives it to **Amy***. She looks inside. She takes out two tickets.*

Alan (*almost amused*)   Aruba?

Stephen *shrugs.* **Amy** *looks to* **Alan***.*

Alan (*laughs, relieved*)   Nicola! Come in! Stephen's going to the West Indies!

Amy   There's two tickets here, Stephen.

Stephen (*to* **Alan**)   How's she been, by the way? Looking after her?

Alan   I thought that you told me your time was short, Stephen.

Stephen (*amused*)   I did? Did I say that? Well, one can only assume I've had a new lease of life, yes?

Alan*'s had enough. He approaches* **Stephen***.*

Stephen   Oh now, come on. Don't look at me like that. I came to my senses after a few scoops, didn't I? I would hardly think you have much right to talk. Well, by the look of you, anyway. You think that us drunkards are the only ones who're compulsive?

Alan   Let me show you the door.

Stephen   Got a bit of a limp there, son.

Alan   Pick up your hat.

Stephen You wouldn't have an odd packet of those luxury crisps, would you?

Alan (*angry*) I said, 'Pick up your hat,' Stephen. Pick it up and . . . get lost, all right?

Stephen *just smiles at him.* **Alan** *growls in anger. He picks up* **Stephen**'s *hat and offers it to him.* **Stephen** *turns to* **Amy**. **Alan** *throws the hat down.*

Amy Stephen, you can't possibly be expecting that I'm going to come with you. (*Regarding tickets.*) How . . . how on earth did you afford these?

Stephen How do you think I afforded them?

Amy *looks at him, clueless.*

Stephen Credit cards!

Amy You stole somebody's credit cards?

Stephen What would I want to steal them for, woman? When they're giving them away! (*Regarding* **Alan**, *to* **Amy**.) Hmm. Let me guess: he's on Prozac, yes?

Alan (*enraged, confronting him*) She's not going to Aruba! She's not going anywhere. The woman's getting a job: she has a future, good prospects!

Stephen (*surprised*) A job?

Alan Are you deaf?

Stephen *looks at* **Amy** *a moment. He laughs uproariously. He takes out his hip-flask. He uncaps it. He takes a drink. He notices* **Alan** *is staring at him.*

Stephen (*good-natured*) Like a drop?

Alan Oh, here we go again, the Great God bloody Bacchus?

Stephen The gods are dead, son. Or banished, at least. (*Beat, to* **Amy**.) So, to recap: we fly the coop, as I said, live it up like kings a while, limbo-dancing, tequila . . . and after that, well . . . (*Thinks.*) Well, we'll burn that . . . bridge when we come to her. A birth and a death, Amy. A resurrection.

Alan   A resurrection?

Stephen (*to* **Amy**)   Come with me!

Amy   I . . . I can't just come with you, Stephen. You'd be a fugitive.

Stephen   On a breach of the peace charge? So much for divine justice . . . (*Beat.*) Terrible, of course, how things turned out. And to think we came so close to solving the mystery. Oh well. At least they can explain it away with the binge-drinking, huh?

Alan   There was nothing in that damn car, Stephen.

Stephen (*shrugs*)   You're sure of that, are you? (*Wickedly.*) You didn't split the winnings?

Amy (*sternly*)   Leave it, Stephen.

Stephen   Fair enough, fair enough. (*Sadly.*) In a way, I suppose, it isn't really my business. We think addiction's the problem. While the truth simply is . . . (*Beat.*) What we simply want is . . . anaesthesia. Medication by night, and moral instruction. (*Laughs.*) Of course, if we'd happened by chance to see the true bacchanal, if we'd stumbled upon the heart of the mystery . . . (*Laughs.*) Well, to be honest with you, I . . .

Alan (*coldly*)   And what's the 'true' bacchanal?

Stephen (*laughs*)   Oh, I'm sure you wouldn't be interested.

Alan   Amuse me.

Stephen   Well, it was like I told that bewildered young soul in that bar of yours, wasn't it? It's the search for oneself. The god becoming man. The god passing through him. The hooves thundering by: the water and wind. For all of the masks are stripped away then, aren't they? (*Laughs.*) To experience that. I don't think the folks could take it.

He turns to **Amy**. *He looks at her. He sighs. He picks up his hat.*

Stephen   Very well. Very well. I have made my petition. There's not much else I can do, is there? But I regret to inform

you I shall be leaving on Thursday, and from that day forth
you shall not see me again. (*Laughs.*) I mean, I've heard it said:
you can't serve God and Mammon. But when the shit hits the
fan, who takes the rap, huh?

He drinks again. He toasts them.

Well. It's been fun.

He hesitates. He gives **Amy** *one final look. He goes off.*

Amy (*embarrassed*)   Stephen.

Alan   I think I said it before. You know how to pick them.

Amy   He was funny, at least. I mean, he was always that.

Silence.

Oh, Stephen!

Alan (*indignant*)   How the hell can he have known that we
have luxury crisps?

Amy *looks at him a moment. She does not know this person. She goes off.*

Alan (*a sudden panic*)   Amy!

He is struck by a tremor. It terrifies him. He steadies himself.

Oh, you mother!

He's anxious now.

Nicola, I . . . Stephen's leaving, all right? Stephen's leaving just
now – in a couple of minutes. Everything's going to be fine,
we've just got one more thing to discuss here.

He goes to the phone. He picks it up. He takes a deep breath. He dials.

(*Into phone.*) Richard. Hello. Richard. Yes, I got your message.
No problem. No problem. Well, what time do you want me to
drive down there, then? (*Beat.*) Yeah. Okay. (*Beat.*) No, that's
cool. I'll see you tomorrow then, Richard.

He puts the phone down. He is struck by another tremor.

Nicola!

Nicola *comes on.*

Nicola   There's no need to holler, babe: I'm not far away. (*She looks about.*) Gone, at last, have they? Well, thank the good Lord for that. I was going stir-crazy in there.

Alan   Tell me about it!

Silence.

Nicola   You think she'll go for that job, then? I mean, I know it's a long shot.

Alan   I think they're going to Aruba.

Nicola (*laughs*)   Excuse me?

Alan   Stephen's going to Aruba.

Nicola   Well, you said it yourself, Alan, the woman has problems.

Alan   It's not like she can tell me that I didn't try, right?

Nicola *looks at* **Alan**.

Nicola   Are you sure you're okay?

She approaches him, concerned.

Alan (*laughs*)   I'm great, never better. I was just admiring . . . the bowl of stones.

He looks at her a moment. He smiles, defeated. He looks over the balcony.

I'm thinking it's about time I bought myself a car.

She takes his hand. They both look over the balcony.

She takes her sunglasses off her head, and puts them over her eyes.

Both remain standing, hand in hand, staring at the sunset.

Lights down slowly.